When God Stops Fighting

When God Stops Fighting

HOW RELIGIOUS VIOLENCE ENDS

Mark Juergensmeyer

 UNIVERSITY OF CALIFORNIA PRESS

University of California Press
Oakland, California

© 2022 by Mark Juergensmeyer

Library of Congress Cataloging-in-Publication Data

Names: Juergensmeyer, Mark, author.
Title: When God stops fighting : how religious violence ends / Mark
    Juergensmeyer.
Description: [Oakland, California] : [University of California Press],
    [2022] | Includes bibliographical references and index..
Identifiers: LCCN 2021021120 (print) | LCCN 2021021121 (ebook) |
    ISBN 9780520384729 (hardcover) | ISBN 9780520384736 (paperback) |
    ISBN 9780520384743 (ebook)
Subjects: LCSH: Violence—Religious aspects—Islam. | Violence—Iraq—
    Religious aspects. | Violence—Philippines—Religious aspects. |
    Violence—India—Punjab—Religious aspects. | Religious militants—
    Interviews. | BISAC: RELIGION / Religion, Politics & State | SOCIAL
    SCIENCE / Violence in Society
Classification: LCC BP190.5.V56 J84 2022 (print) |
    LCC BP190.5.V56 (ebook) | DDC 297.2/7—dc23
LC record available at https://lccn.loc.gov/2021021120
LC ebook record available at https://lccn.loc.gov/2021021121

Manufactured in the United States of America

25 24 23 22 21
10 9 8 7 6 5 4 3 2 1

Contents

Preface

"The war is over," the former ISIS fighter told me. When I talked with him he was incarcerated in a prison in Iraq's Kurdistan region. He had been convicted of being a jihadi warrior with the Islamic State, but now he expressed disillusionment with the movement and its leadership.[1]

I had asked him whether the ISIS struggle was still attractive to some people. He looked at me in disbelief, and then said quietly, "the war is over." Without admitting that he ever was fully in it, he was acknowledging that this battle was now a thing of the past. What he did not admit, however, was that the apocalyptic imagery of conflict at the end times and the rise of a Caliphate was no longer valid. The battle was over, but the ideas remained. It was a sentiment that he shared with many of the old ISIS fighters, as I was to discover in other conversations. Yet for now, he sadly acknowledged, the war was over.

It is not an easy thing to slip out of war. Perhaps it is more difficult than slipping into it, considering all of the personal, social, and spiritual aspects of a commitment to a struggle that have to be abandoned. Yet war ends. Violent movements, even those informed by religious visions of great warfare, terminate, or are transformed into more peaceful elements within the broader society.

In this book I want to try to understand how this happens. My motive is to complete my own understanding of the rise of movements of religious nationalism and religion-related violence around the world, a project in which I have been engaged for decades. The natural conclusion of these studies is to understand how such movements end. As it turns out, it is also a timely one.

As I prepared this book for publication, the news media fixated on the assault on the US Capitol building on January 6, 2021, provoked by then-president Donald Trump. Though not overtly religious, the White supremacists who were among the most ardent members of that insurrection privileged Christian culture. The conspiratorial mythology of the QAnon movement to which many of the participants adhered borrowed heavily from the imagery and end-times rhetoric of millenarian evangelical Protestant Christianity. Many of the participants regarded their involvement as part of a godly crusade—the kind of cosmic war that is in the minds of similar religious activists of various faiths around the world who see worldly confrontations as expressions of a metaphysical struggle between good and evil, right and wrong.

It is of timely importance then, to understand not only how such movements arise—the mood of alienation and marginalization that has propelled people to imagine themselves in a great righteous war—but also how they might end. As the case studies in this book will indicate, the way that governmental authorities respond to these movements can make all the difference. It can exacerbate the situation or alleviate it. But such movements do end.

To understand how this happens, I've tried to get inside the minds and mindsets of individuals involved in specific cases. I have chosen case studies where violent movements have largely come to a close. In deciding on which cases to focus I considered a range of possibilities. I could have chosen the Protestant-Catholic conflict in Northern Ireland, though I have elsewhere already analyzed how this conflict ended.[2] Or I could have examined the Lord's Resistance Army in Uganda, though that movement, even in a diminished state, continues its savage warfare in the region. The list of cases of terminated struggles goes on, though many imagined wars are still continuing and it is too early to examine how they might end.

Out of the range of possibilities I have chosen three case studies, selected in part because they show the range of possibilities in bringing violent movements to a close. One of them is the Islamic State, based in Iraq and Syria, which reigned over large sections of both countries from 2015 to 2017 and was territorially defeated by 2019. This is a movement that I have studied since its inception, through multiple visits to the region, and is an example of attempts to crush such uprisings through military destruction.

The second case is the Moro Movement for a Muslim Mindanao in the southern Philippines, a Muslim separatist movement that persisted from 1969 to 2019, when a peace agreement was finally ratified by a plebiscite in the region. This was a new movement for me to study, but I chose it in part because it showed the possibilities of the transition from violence to nonviolence through skillful negotiation—much like the Northern Ireland case.

The third case I have chosen is the Khalistan movement for Sikh separatism in the north Indian state of Punjab. The Sikh movement was involved in a deadly conflict with the Indian government throughout the 1980s and finally came to an end in 1995 for a variety of reasons, including an all-out assault by the Indian police.

This is a movement that I know well, since I lived for a time in the region, and it was the rise of religious nationalism in the 1980s in the Punjab that first sparked my interest in studying the relationship between religion and nationalism in strident new movements of opposition. It also interested me because it was an example, like ISIS, of militant suppression, but also of the collapse of popular support for the uprising. Hence these three cases provided me with a range of ways in which violent movements end.

I realize that in choosing two Muslim cases out of the three I may be giving a false impression that Islam is more prone to violence and movements of religious nationalism than other religious traditions. This is not the case. For a more balanced view of the rise of religious violence that occurs in all religious traditions one may consult my earlier books, *Global Rebellion: Religious Nationalism Confronts the Secular State,* and *Terror in the Mind of God: The Global Rise of Religious Violence.*[3] For this book, I have chosen these two cases because they provide an interesting comparison with each other and with the Khalistan case regarding how such movements end.

I say that each of these movements came to an end, though in each case aspects of the struggle linger on. Occasional acts of violence associated with them continue. Moreover, like the former ISIS soldier I met, the sense of militancy, the vision of great war, that animated each of them has endured among some supporters. Among many others, however, the idea of war was over long before the hostilities ended. That loss of faith in the war effort may have been a major factor in the ending of each of these movements.

How much of a factor was it? This is what I wanted to find out by looking more closely at each of these cases. I have traveled to these three regions on multiple occasions over several years and talked with a variety of former supporters and others knowledgeable about the situation. By looking at different cases I hoped to find elements that were common to all three, as well as those that were not. I hoped to develop the range of patterns regarding how visions of warfare come to an end. I also wanted to understand what factors propelled the movement towards abandoning the idea of war, factors that were both internal to the movement and that came from outside, including the actions of government authorities who were trying to control or crush the movements. Which of these actions were helpful in bringing an end to the hostilities and which were counter-productive?

This book is the culmination of thirty years of studying the rise of religious violence around the world, a project that has resulted in a series of books. The first was *The New Cold War? Religious Nationalism Confronts the Secular State,* published in 1993; it has been revised, expanded, and re-issued as *Global Rebellion.*[4] This book explored the rise of movements of religious nationalism around the world; it found similarities in the loss of faith in secular nationalism, and attempts to recreate national community through ethnic and religious loyalties.

The next book in this series was *Terror in the Mind of God.* This focused on the violence often associated with the rise of strident new movements of religious nationalism, including disturbing acts of public violence characterized as terrorism. The book surveyed such movements in every religious tradition, and found similarities in their use of acts of terrorism as performance violence, symbolic empowerment, and imagined cosmic wars.

Though in some ways the present book, *When God Stops Fighting,* is the completion of this trilogy, two other books of mine helped to illumine aspects of the phenomenon of religious violence and nationalism. One was a co-authored work based on a five-year Luce

Foundation-funded project assessing the role of religion in public life around the globe. This book, *God in the Tumult of the Global Square: Religion in Global Civil Society*, found similarities among different forms of public religion in both destructive and positive ways.[5] It showed that even religious authority has eroded in the global age and explored the potential for a global civil religion.

A direct companion to the current volume is *God at War: A Meditation on Religion and Warfare*.[6] In fact, that book began as the opening chapter of the book you are reading now, *When God Stops Fighting*. I wanted to explain how religion was related to imagined wars in order to understand how those images could be domesticated and contained. But the more I thought about it the chapter became a separate book, based in part on lectures I had given on the topic at Princeton and Muenster. *God at War* explored two basic impulses of the human imagination, the longing for religion and the tendency to war, and tried to understand what they have in common. These impulses are sometimes fused in the minds of those who have imagined apocalyptic images of cosmic war. It is this kind of heightened religious warfare that I have found to be frequently the mental template that accompanies violent acts related to religion.

How can these images of warfare be ameliorated? How can confidence in them erode, and how can those who gain power by conducting them be seen as less legitimate? These are some of the questions behind the present book. As I have said, it is in some ways the culmination of a series of works in which I have tried to understand how and why imagined warfare has emerged as a global phenomenon at this moment of history, and what religion has to do with it. Now the time has come to try to understand how these movements wind down and how their visions of grand warfare are abandoned.

In working on this project I have been indebted to the "Resolving Jihadist Conflicts" project hosted by the Department of Peace and Conflict Research at Uppsala University, Sweden. I have appreciated its support for travel and research, and been stimulated by the interaction with my team members, Mimmi Söderberg Kovaks, Desirée Nilsson, Ebrahim Moosa, Emin Poljarevic, and Mona Kanwal Sheikh, as well as the able director of the project, Isak Svensson.

With regard to the ISIS case, in several trips to Kurdistan and elsewhere in Northern Iraq I appreciated the arrangements and translation assistance of Ibrahim Anli and Dilshad Ahmad at Ishik University, Erbil; Rabeen Fadhil of the Middle East Dialogue Center, Erbil; and Shahid Burhan Hadi from Suliamaniya. Monitoring online jihadi conversations with ISIS supporters on social media was conducted by my diligent research assistants Mufid Taha and Saba Sadri.

In the Philippines I was grateful for the support and hospitality of the faculty and staff of Notre Dame University, Cotabato City, especially the Vice-President for Administration, Sheila Algabre, and the President (before 2018), Fr. Charlie M. Inzon, OMI, and (after 2018), Fr. Francis Zabala, OMI. In Manila, Mike Saycon was helpful in providing contacts, and the fluent Tagalog of my colleague Collin Dvorak proved to be invaluable.

In India, I relied on my old Punjabi friends, including Harish Puri, Mohinder Singh, and Gurinder Singh Mann, for contacts in the Punjab and elsewhere. In Amritsar, Jagrup Singh Sekhon was generous in his time and expertise in accompanying me on research visits to meet with former militants. Paul Wallace was gracious in providing me copies of his reports and publications on the uprising. In the Punjab, as in all three cases, I am deeply appreciative of all those whom I met for taking time to talk with me and being so open in sharing with me their perspectives on the rise and fall of religious-related violent movements in their regions.

I am grateful for the University of California Press for taking this project on, as it has for many of the other books I have published on this topic. I appreciate the role of Eric Schmidt in shepherding it through the publication process. And as always I am grateful for the support of my friend and spouse, Sucheng Chan, whose own writing is a model of elegance and clarity. She endured my frequent research trips, sometimes wondering if I would ever return. I hope that she will feel that it was all worthwhile.

In this book I want to bring the reader with me into the worlds imagined by supporters of each of these three movements. We will try to understand how sensible people could be drawn into a state of remarkable war, and how in time they lost faith in that vision and found ways to extricate themselves from the movements that had fostered it. It will be a remarkable journey to three quite different locales, but in each case the end will be the promise of enduring peace.

1   *The Trajectory of Imagined Wars*

"Maybe the war is over," one of the former militants in the Moro separatist movement in the Philippines told me. The hesitancy in his optimism reflected the uncertainties in the peace process between the Philippine government and the main militant movement, the Moro Islamic Liberation Front. A peace agreement that had been negotiated in 2015 was finally signed by President Rodrigo Duterte in 2018 after years of stalling that fueled the opposition and led to a major military confrontation in the city of Marawi in 2017. So despite the continuing tension, he now had reason to at least hope that the war was coming to an end.

What he meant by the ending of the war was not just a matter of militants in his movement capitulating to the overwhelming strength of the Philippine government and laying down their arms. He meant a change in attitude towards the conflict. He was talking about the shift in worldviews from a situation of absolute opposition to one where opponents were not foes. They were not yet friends, but there was now the potential for a working arrangement in which they would be able to negotiate differences and build a common future.

That was a big change indeed. If the peace process holds in the Philippines—and it is still a big "if"—it will be an interesting example of how the warfare that characterizes terrorism comes to an end. In this case, it will end relatively peacefully. If the peace process does not hold, however, there might be a revival of Moro separatist militancy.

Outside Mosul in Northern Iraq, a young Sunni Arab with whom I spoke was more confident. Looking back at the years under the rule of the Islamic State, he said, "we were constantly at war." He described the reign of terror under which Mosul was controlled until the city was liberated by coalition forces early in 2017. "But now," he added, "it's over."

When I interviewed him in a refugee camp near the destroyed village of Hasan Sham at the outskirts of Mosul he was still recounting the terror of the years under the movement's control and the nightmare of battle in the days leading up to the liberation of the city. Though he professed that the war was over, clearly the memory of it was indelibly on his mind.

He admitted that initially most of his Sunni Arab neighbors bought into the idea of war propounded by the Islamic State, also known as ISIS or ISIL. He and his neighbors thought that the movement would empower Sunnis in a post-Saddam Iraq skewed towards Shi'a control. He would not say whether he was a supporter or member of the movement, but his silence on that topic was powerful. As the years wore on and ISIS became even more brutal and indiscriminate in its victims, many former supporters lost faith in the regime, became disillusioned with its war, and began to silently turn against it. When they had the chance they willingly fled from its control. For him, the terror of the imagined war of the Islamic State was now a thing of the past, though the reality of it was only slowly beginning to recede.

"The war never really ended," one of the former militants in India's Khalistan movement told me when I met with him in his village in the state of Punjab. He added that "it simply went underground." By "underground," he meant not a guerilla movement, but the harboring of images of great struggle and conquest among old warriors who still felt that the conflict was not resolved. The actual fighting—the terror and the brutal killing on both sides of the conflict—ended in the 1990s. Other observers and some of the former militants told me that the violence had indeed ended, and that there would never be another bloody uprising like that one that gripped the region during the 1980s. The costs to the local citizenry were just too high. But because many of the issues were unresolved, there were rumblings about the movement being revived.

What interested me about the Khalistan case and the other two cases that I examine in this book—the Muslim movement for a separate Mindanao in the Philippines and the Islamic State regime in Iraq and Syria—is how diverse were the attitudes of the participants in the struggles. The former fighters not only viewed their battles differently, but also saw the endings of the movements from differing perspectives. Sometimes they accepted that the end was marked with military defeat; in other cases they hoped that the resolution would allow them to integrate into society again. But to a large extent they acknowledged that the central ideas undergirding the struggle had collapsed, and the image of an all-or-nothing conflict with an impossible enemy dissipated or was transformed into a non-physical form of conflict. How is it possible that this notion of absolute warfare, so all-consuming and central to the leitmotif of a movement, could come to an end?

I think the answers to this question are essential in helping us understand how participants in violent movements throughout the world have abandoned their struggles. Negotiation is not possible until both sides have lost the will to fight. Military conquests work only if the surviving antagonists in the conflict give up the struggle and do not choose to continue it in some other way, such as through guerilla warfare or sporadic acts of terrorism. At the heart of the transformation from militancy to the cessation of hostilities is the abandonment of the idea of war, at least at it relates to the conduct of war.

It might not be easy for combatants to doff this idea. If the struggle has persisted over many years, those fighting may have become accustomed to war as the normal way of viewing the world. In some cases their careers may depend on it. Some fighters have known only war, and their personal achievements and social recognition may be tied to their roles as soldiers in a great battle. To give up the idea of war, for many fighters, means a transformation in the way they think about themselves and their place in the world.

Moreover, when religion is part of the ideology of violent movements, the image of warfare may be fused in some way with a grand vision of metaphysical struggle. To abandon such images, then, involves not only a strategic choice about a movement's engagement and a personal change in the lives of many of its fighting supporters, but a transformation of faith. Just as a conversion into a religious war worldview was the occasion for many supporters to join a movement, the abandonment of this worldview will require a conversion out of it, or a dramatic accommodation to a new sense of nonviolent religious commitment.

This brings up a larger question that is relevant in each of these cases. They all are about violent movements, to be sure, and they all are identified in some way with religion. But the way that the violence is related to religion is not the same in each instance, nor is it the same for all supporters of the movement, nor does it stay the same through the duration of the movement. When we look at each case we will try to identify these differences. For now, however, it is useful to think a bit about what we mean by war and how religion can be related to it.

Imagined War and Absolute War

When the young Sunni Arab man I interviewed in a refugee camp near Mosul said that he thought that ISIS was constantly in a state of war, just what did he mean by that? You could say that Sunni Arabs in Iraq have been in conflict with the majority Shi'a ever since the end of the Saddam regime. They have resisted the American military, seen as propping up the Shi'a government. So when the young man in the refugee camp talked about the ISIS view of war, was he just talking about conflicting positions, or did he mean something more than that? Just what did he mean by "war"?

The way that war is conceived is not always the same, and the way that religion relates to it differs as well. In a companion volume to this book, *God at War*, I look at some of these differences.[1] Here, I'll give you a brief rundown of its most relevant conclusions. The idea of war, I've found, is more than a matter of conflicting points of views. It embraces the notion of an absolute conflict with a moral valence, a do-or-die struggle between good and evil. It involves a totally new way of looking at the world, the very opposite of civil society, where differences are mediated by law and negotiation. In war there are only the good guys and the bad guys, and the bad guys are hell-bent on destroying the good guys. Those at war invariably think that they are the good guys.

This radically upside-down war worldview is, in large part, a reaction to existential fear. When I looked at the way that war springs into the imagination of people at the onset of a military encounter, I discovered that it is in many ways a response to a social anomaly—the feeling that things are deeply awry, and that something sinister must have caused it. This applies to the collapse of the World Trade Center at 9/11, and it also applies to the Sunni Arab fear that in a post-Saddam world their lives and their culture would be forever altered, and they were going to be treated as second-class citizens or worse.

War gives voice to these fears. It provides a conceptual framework in which these social disasters make sense. A devious enemy devised them, the victims think, and unless they engage the enemy in an all-out winner-take-all confrontation, the enemy will make matters even worse. Thus the idea of war gives conceptual clarity to humiliating and destructive events and situations. And it provides a solution—military engagement and the expectation of victory. The victims of these disasters do not need to sit passively by and watch their worst fears realized; they can fight back. They can become soldiers in an awesome war.

So in that sense every war is an imagined war. It is a way of trying to come to grips with an awful situation. To some extent many, if not most, wars are also real, of course, in that there are often identifiable and actual opponents. They may indeed act like enemies, the cause of the problems of the other side, and they may indeed have sinister motives and devious tactics for doing the other side in. But at other times it is not clear who the enemy is or whether that enemy is aware of how they are perceived. Yet thinking of them as the enemy enables the possibility of war; it helps to clarify things in the mind of those who deem themselves oppressed. It provides a conceptual template of understanding in which one can understand the role of an enemy—either real or fabricated—and what the appropriate response should be. Usually it is to fight like hell. The concept of war magnifies a community's fears into a worldview of absolute opposition.

In the case of the Sunni Arabs, it was clear that the Shi'a were indeed usurping the Sunnis' accustomed roles of political leadership in Iraq, and they were correct in thinking that these developments would lead to the marginalization of Sunni Arabs. In the case of 9/11 the enemy was not so clear—some Americans thought it was just the small cadre of jihadists who plotted the attack, while others identified the whole Muslim world as the enemy. In the Philippine struggle, the Mindanao Muslims had a clear enemy: the government that was not giving them separatist identity and power. The enemy in the case of Khalistan in India was less clear, sometimes appearing to be the government and the police, sometimes Hindu and moderate Sikhs who opposed the movement. When the enemy is not obvious, it might have to be conjured up.

As I will explain later in this chapter, there are occasions when dramatic threats and social discord raise in the public mind the idea that war may be afoot, that the chaos is part of some evil plot to undergird society. This may indeed be the case, but even if it is not, this notion of war requires that there be some sort of enemy who might have caused the discord. Hence, in some cases, to sustain the idea of war enemies have to be invented.

Here's where religion often comes into the picture. Religious culture can be of service to the idea of war by helping to create an enemy: someone who is not part of the militants' religious community, for example, or a secular political order that is by its nature non-religious, and behind them perhaps Satan himself. Religious ideas and images can also be of service in helping to legitimize the fight, to imply that this is not just a contest between two equally moral sides, but a battle where one side is favored by God. The invariable implication, from the point of view of those imaging a treacherous enemy, is that God is on their side.

This religious legitimization is especially important in cases where military combat is not just a matter of trying to gain or defend territory, or achieve a specific policy objection, but also when it is a matter of obliterating an enemy thought to be devious by its very nature. This kind of war is what the theorist of warfare, Carl von Clausewitz, called "absolute war." The nineteenth-century Prussian soldier is famous for one line from his posthumously published manual *On War*, the-oft quoted sentence that "war is the continuation of politics by other means."[2] Yet this famous phrase is taken out of context. If you read the whole thing, you will see that the idea that war is politics by other means is simply the way that war tends to be conducted by most states in most cases. It is not war in its essence. For that Clausewitz coined a much more interesting phrase, "absolute war" or "ideal war." This phrase describes how war is imagined, more than how it is actually conducted. It is the most extreme form of war, one that aims solely at the destruction of the other side, the absolute defeat of the enemy by whatever means.

It is this notion of war that Clausewitz thinks is behind all versions of warfare, including the carefully controlled and targeted versions that are meant for policy purposes as "politics by other means." Yet occasionally this politically-controlled warfare gets out of hand, reverting to its true nature of an all-or-nothing combat between enemies each of which is pledged to do the other in, totally and without mercy. In these cases of absolute warfare religion can play a significant role. It can provide the aura of religiosity that makes such savage attacks morally comprehensible. At the extreme end is a form of absolute war that is totally merged with a religious view of the world. It is this form of religious warfare that I've called "cosmic war."

Religion and War

In my book *God at War,* I've tried to explain how this fusion of religion and warfare is possible.[3] I have suggested that all war is in a sense imagined war, in that the idea of war is a powerful prerequisite to actual military implementation, and in fact makes it possible. This imagined war can be characterized as an alternative reality, since it describes not just an encounter with an enemy but also a worldview in which the major elements of social reality are located. It is an inversion of ordinary reality where differences are negotiated through civil discourse and a respect for opponents even when you disagree with them. War turns that social reality on its head. In the war worldview there is a stark, dichotomous distinction between us and them, the good guys and the bad ones. The alternative reality of war turns normal civil order upside down as the war worldview allows for a centralized autocratic leadership to totally crush an evil opposition.

What interests me about war's relation to religion is not only the way that war uses religion, and religion uses war, but how sometimes the two are fused. Religion is also an alternative reality. Like war, it imagines a completely different way of looking at the world, one in which there are spiritual forces at work and individuals are able to tap into this power by transcending ordinary reality and shifting into a spiritual dimension of life. Just as the worldview of war provides a way of making sense of social chaos, explaining and encountering a world gone awry, the religious worldview does much the same thing. In the case of religion, though, it is not just a social anomaly that is encountered but an intensely personal one, the confrontation with the notion of mortality and the reality of one's own impending death. Religion, like war, can take the fear of discord and not only mask it but provide a template for action in which one can overcome the forces that lead to the discord, and thus banish the fear.

So religion and war are competing alternative realities, though they can also be compatible. War uses religion to legitimize its worldview, and borrows from religious images of warfare its own attempts to force one side's moral claims upon the other. After 9/11, in the social disruption and state of conceptual chaos that confused many Americans, it was not just an image of warfare—"the global war on terror"—that was a comforting conceptual response, but also the assurance that God was on America's side. "God Bless America," said the banners and bumperstickers in the bellicose spirit of the time.

On the other hand, religion uses war. For the most part it uses war metaphorically, to speak of the conflict between good and evil that is part of the spiritual life. When pious Protestant Christians sing the hymn "Onward Christian Soldiers, Marching as to War," seldom do they think they they are entering into a real military encounter using swords and sub-machine guns. They think of the war *within*, just as most pious Muslims regard *jihad*, "struggle," as an internal and spiritual conflict and not an engagement with a real political foe. It is true that religious scriptures are saturated with bloodshed. The great Hindu epics, the *Mahabharata* and the *Ramayana*, are full of gory battles. Some of the most popular television programs in India have been serialized versions of these epic battle stories. But few people in India think that these epic battles are being waged today. Rather these accounts are taken to be testaments to the faith and a lesson about God's loyalty to those who follow him, much like the warfare and destruction portrayed in the Hebrew Bible, revered by Jews, Muslims, and Christians, where in Exodus and Deuteronomy God is pictured as a military commander who shows no mercy and takes no prisoners. Few readers take this literally.

So war and religion can use each other, as often they do. But what if the alternative realities are fused together, and religion is thought to be war, and war religion? This describes some of the most vicious movements of religious violence in recent years, including the apocalyptic vision that was fundamental to the views of the leaders of ISIS. The ISIS religious/political worldview admittedly was extreme. But this view of religious warfare has been a remarkably common feature of many of the movements of religious violence in recent years.

The Fusion of Alternative Realities: Cosmic War

I have called this merger of the alternative realities of religion and warfare "cosmic war," an idea that is central to many strident religiously-related movements around the world, including to some extent the three that are the case studies of this book.[4] It is "cosmic" because it imagines the true confrontation behind worldly clashes to be on a transhistorical and metaphysical level. It is conducted with an uncompromising absolutism similar to the idea of Clausewitz's notion of "absolute war." In merging absolute war with religion, cosmic war often appropriates traditional images of *holy war,* imagining that God is guiding military engagements that ultimately are waged on a transcendent spiritual plane. Needless to say, this kind of belief about war is difficult to combat. It gives an illusion of invulnerability to the warriors who ascribe to it, and an uncompromising attitude to leaders who have no patience with negotiation. Those who engage in it imagine themselves as religious soldiers who are fighting for God and who can literally stave off the forces of evil.

The image of cosmic war is a potent force. When the template of spiritual battle is implanted onto worldly oppositions it dramatically alters the way that the struggles are perceived and waged. When a confrontation is deemed to be a cosmic war it is thought to be conducted both on a mortal and a transcendent scale where normal timelines have no meaning. Years ago, when I had the opportunity to interview the political head of the Hamas movement in Gaza, I asked him how he thought Hamas could defeat the Israeli military, one of the most powerful fighting forces in the Middle East, with only car bombs and suicide attacks. He looked at me thoughtfully, and then, as if speaking to a small child, he said, "Maybe not in my lifetime, nor even in my children's lifetime, or even in my children's children's lifetime, but maybe," he said, pausing for effect, "in my children's children's children's lifetime we might win." Then he explained, "This is God's war, not ours. We cannot lose."[5]

Conceiving of a conflict as God's war does change the equation for those who are engaged in it. For one thing, they know that whatever they do, ultimately they will not lose. So even if a skirmish with the enemy almost entirely obliterates their own fighting force, they know that they may have lost this battle but they will win the war. "It is God's war," they think, and like the Hamas leader, they believe that therefore they cannot lose.

This means that soldiers in a cosmic war are always buoyed by the notion that they are on the victorious side. Their engagement in it is personal. The very act of fighting in God's war is redemptive, an act of service to God, and if one is maimed or killed in the process this is the ultimate personal offering, an act of martyrdom that glorifies the soul. Some Muslims believe that martyrdom will give them heavenly rewards, though the notion that seventy-two virgins await each martyr is an interpretation that is not substantiated by the Qur'an. It does mention *houris,* beings to comfort all who are in heaven, but these are not specifically for martyrs nor even specifically for men, much less for sexual purposes. Even so, the act of martyrdom, in Islam as in Christianity, is something that is spiritually meritorious. Being engaged in God's war can bring salvation.

Thinking of war in cosmic terms also changes the way one perceives the enemy. Like all war this perspective absolutizes the conflict into extreme opposing positions, but it goes further by demonizing opponents. It imagines them to be satanic powers. These enemies become devils by necessity, since one cannot imagine a war in cosmic terms without a satanic foe. The image of the enemy as the source of all evil is a fiction created by the requirements of cosmic war. In fact, one cannot conceive of a cosmic war without it. The satanic opposing army would have to be invented if it did not already exist.

This brings up an interesting point to which I have alluded earlier: inventing enemies. Our common sense notion is that people go to war because they have enemies. But if one conceives of the world being in the grips of a cosmic war, one has to identify real-world enemies as if they are cosmic foes. Groups that may be disliked for one reason or other, or deemed oppressive, may be reconceived as agents of transcendent satanic powers. When the idea of cosmic war occurs—and it often does so suddenly, in a kind of conversion experience—the beholder sees the world with fresh eyes, and perceives familiar opponents to be darker visages of the evil other. Any notion of war can change one's view of reality. Cosmic war changes it in ways that incorporate myth and legend and a transcendent view of ultimate metaphysical conflict.

Non-War, War, and Cosmic War

In the three case studies in this book, I will be mindful of these distinctions among the kinds of warfare we have discussed: war using religion, religion using war, and cosmic war merging religion and war. A conflict begins to turn into war when it becomes increasingly absolutized. Opponents are thought to be impossible foes, enemies with whom one cannot easily negotiate or engage civilly. Violent encounter is perceived to be the only option in a contestation of force.

War often becomes permeated with religion. If not at the outset, at some point in its progress, supporters of a war effort will begin to apply religious elements to it. It will be seen as supported by God, and blessings will be given to those fighting it. Religious language and images will give credibility to the struggle and a sense of virtue to those who are involved in what is, after all, publicly sanctioned murder—the act of killing in warfare.

At some point in the struggle the conflict may be conceived in even grander terms, as cosmic war. This is when God is seen not just as favoring a human effort, but conducting it. It becomes "God's war," as the Hamas political leader told me. Though enemies are caricatured in any view of war, in cosmic war they are satanized in a way that makes it impossible to imagine settling with them, or conceiving that they could change. A mortal enemy can change and become the kind of adversary with whom one can compromise and negotiate, and among whom one could imagine eventually peaceably co-existing. But there's no negotiating with an agent of Satan.

Eventually, however, wars come to an end. Even cosmic wars dissolve into history. Often, the ending of war is simply non-war. I would like to call it peace, but that term implies a resolution of the underlying conflictual issues and an ability of former combatants to accept each other with tolerance and magnanimity. I suppose that can happen, but in most of the cases that I am exploring in this book what happens is a cessation of hostilities, a state of non-war. It is not peace, in the sense of friendly toleration of the other; hatreds may continue to abound. But at least people are not killing each other.

So in these case studies I want to explore the trajectory of movements of religious violence. I want to look at the transitions of worldviews, if there are any, to see how, for example, a state of non-war moves to war, war to cosmic war, and cosmic war back to non-war. I say this is one example, since I do not expect the trajectory of transitions to be the same in every case. Nor do I expect that the experience is the same for all engaged in these movements; some leaders may see the conflict as cosmic war, while some foot soldiers may see it as an ordinary struggle to secure benefits for themselves and their communities. For the purpose of this book, I am particularly interested in how things move in reverse, how a grand image of cosmic war decays as its adherents begin to see the struggle in more mortal terms, and how conflict even during hostilities can still be negotiated. In some instances, the image of cosmic war may persist to the end before it collapses, in other cases there may be a slow erosion of commitment before it finally becomes transformed into more manageable forms of opposition.

The case studies in this book are all instances in which the idea of cosmic war has become fixated in the minds of many engaged in a religiously-related social conflict, and they are all cases in which that idea changes or ends. I will try to understand what elements, both internal and external to the movements, have been conducive to this transformation. The movements could be affected by changing dynamics within their organizations or by shifting responses of government authorities to what they perceive as terrorist threats. Yet even without these changes, there can be a fundamental altering or rejecting of images of cosmic war. We know that such visions of cosmic war can rise up suddenly with striking popular force. Can they end equally as suddenly, and if so, how?

My hunch is that images of cosmic war finally end when the conditions that led to a sense of frustration and humiliation among those who subscribed to a cosmic-war worldview are altered, or when the fictional construct of cosmic war no longer seems viable. In order to understand what measures lead to these changes in attitude and the diminishment of images of cosmic war, we will have to enter the worlds and the worldview of ISIS in Iraq, the Moro movement in Mindanao, and the Khalistan movement in India's Punjab. In the chapters that follow you will travel with me to these regions, examine the case studies, and meet with people related to the movements and affected by them to understand how their worldviews can change.

2 *The Apocalyptic War of the Islamic State*

I came across these two guys quite by chance. It was shortly after the final days of conflict in the liberation of Mosul from ISIS control in 2017. They were among the thousands of refugees who had fled the city and were now living in one of the enormous camps that had sprung up in the Kurdistan region adjacent to Mosul. I was in the Hasan Sham camp, where the UN High Commission for Refugees, in conjunction with the Kurdish Barzani Foundation, had set up neat rows of one-room tents, arranged in blocks of twenty with bathrooms at each end and common kitchens in the middle. At one side of each block there was an empty lot with water tanks that afforded a few yards of open space. In one of these spaces, plastic chairs had been set up in the dust as a kind of impromptu park. It was there that I encountered these two men.

They were not the ones with whom I had planned to talk. I wanted to find persons who had supported ISIS and who now were reconsidering their pasts. While my Kurdish colleagues were searching to find such persons for me to meet, I struck up a casual conversation with these two fellows who just happened to be next to where I was standing.

Both were good-humored and comfortable talking with me. One, whom I will call Samir, was wearing a typically Arab tunic-style cotton shirt over baggy pants.[1] He was in his early thirties and his tunic attempted to hide a developing pot belly. His friend Ahmad was about the same age, skinnier, sporting a rough beard and a piece of cloth wrapped loosely as a turban, and wearing a leather jacket. He was smoking a cigarette.

I asked them the question that I used to begin most of my interviews in refugee camps: "How did you get here?"

Escape from ISIS

They took turns telling their stories. Samir came from a family of soldiers in Saddam Hussein's old army. After the United States-led military alliance invaded and occupied Iraq in 2003, however, that option was much more difficult for Sunni Arabs like himself, so he applied to the Mosul police force and served as a policeman for several years. Deciding he needed a better income to support his two wives and growing family, he trained himself in plumbing and took up work as an independent contractor. When ISIS took control of Mosul, Samir applied for a position in the waterworks division of the city government, and was hired in the pump maintenance crew.

Ahmad's story was somewhat similar, in that he was also just looking for a job. He came from a village at the outskirts of Mosul, and unlike Samir had no military-style experience. His family were makeshift farmers, selling what they could grow on a few acres, working for larger farms during the harvest season, and tending to cattle at other times. He was able to teach himself carpentry, so after ISIS took control of Mosul he took the opportunity to apply for a division that was responsible for the upkeep and repair of the city's buildings. For a time, he said, life was fairly comfortable.

As we were talking about their roles in the ISIS-controlled city government of Mosul during the early years of the occupation, I was struck with an insight. They could not possibly have gained such positions without some show of support or outright complicity with ISIS. As I mulled this over, I began to realize that I was in fact talking with former ISIS supporters, exactly the kind of people I had hoped to meet. Yet they were now in a refugee camp, seemingly far from their previous lives, and presumably far from ISIS. What had happened?

I asked them whether they had supported ISIS. They hesitated before answering, and then both assured me that they were never soldiers in the ISIS army and were never part of its leadership. That was not exactly what I had asked. But the circumspection of their responses essentially gave me the information that I wanted to know. In one way or another, at least initially during the occupation of Mosul, they must have gotten along well enough with the ISIS ideology and organization.

I tried to word some questions that would get at this association without asking about it directly, since they had already denied any formal connection with the ISIS military. In fact they would be in real trouble if they admitted such ties, since ISIS fighters would be taken out of the general refugee camp, separated into a different section of the camp for detention and interrogation, and in some cases sent off for trial. Long prison sentences awaited them if they were found to have been active ISIS militants.

But these were guys who, they insisted, were not hard-core ISIS militants; they were just trying to get by as best they could in whatever circumstance they found themselves in. That meant that when ISIS seized control of Mosul they went along with whatever they needed to do and say. Was life better under ISIS control of Mosul, I asked them?

Yes, they answered slowly. At least initially, better than before. I probed further, asking in what way their lives had improved. They said that ISIS gave them employment; under Shi'a control their opportunities had been much more limited. They used the term "Shi'a control" rather than Baghdad or the Iraqi government. From their point of view the prejudices of the dominant political power in post-Saddam Iraq were in favor of Shi'a Arabs. That meant that Sunni Arabs in the Western and Northern parts of the country were treated like second-class citizens. They would never have had these opportunities for government jobs before, they said.

I knew enough about the pre-ISIS situation in Mosul to know that what they said was not quite true, for there were many Sunni Arabs employed in government positions in post-Saddam Iraq. Still, their observation had merit; there was a definite pro-Shi'a bias to government hiring and promotion in the years after Saddam. This meant that Samir and Ahmad saw ISIS not only as a radical religious movement but also as a movement for enabling economic opportunities for Sunni Arabs like themselves.

What changed, I asked them. Why did things fall apart? Did ISIS change, or did they change? How had they lost whatever faith they had in the ISIS movement?

Ahmad answered first. It was both, he said. He increasingly felt the loss of personal freedoms. He had loved listening to music on the radio, especially Western popular music, and though they were supposed to turn in their radios when ISIS took control, he kept a small transistor radio under his mattress that could receive music from nearby Kurdistan. He would listen to it very quietly late at night. But he lived in fear of being discovered. Also, he said, he resented having to go to the mosque every week, especially because the imam was an ISIS appointee who would use the opportunity of the sermons to harangue the parishioners with ISIS ideology. This experience poisoned Islam for him, Ahmad said, and he intended never to go to a mosque again the rest of his life. But the most serious problem was his smoking habit. Tobacco was banned under ISIS, but he was still able to find cigarettes through the black market. One day he made the mistake of smoking on the job and one of his superiors reported him to the ISIS morality police. He was fined and put in jail for thirty days, and terminated from his job. After that he tried to eke out an existence doing odd jobs and temporary repairs for individuals.

Samir's explanation was a bit different. Though annoyed by the limitations on personal freedoms, he wasn't restricted by them. But he did see an increasing hardening of ISIS rule, and he placed the blame entirely on its leaders. They got worse, he said, explaining that ISIS leaders had always been paranoid about their imagined enemies. But over time they began turning on their own, infighting within the movement and seeing imagined enemies within the Sunni Arab ranks of their supporters. Samir said that he began to notice that people with whom he worked would be taken off for interrogation from time to time. Some never returned.

One day, Samir said, he himself was called for questioning. A group of ISIS militants surrounded him at work one day and marched him off to a bare government office where he was questioned for hours. Apparently they had found out about his previous employment as a policeman in Mosul. Though Samir did not think that this job made him a government agent, apparently the ISIS interrogators did. They demanded to know why he had not confessed to this earlier. When he could give no acceptable answer he was beaten. Then he was locked up in a cell. He told me that from the moment he was arrested at work he was not able to contact his family, who doubtless were worried about his fate.

The bad situation turned worse a couple days later, he said. ISIS soldiers came to his cell at night, and they yanked him out of his cage. They forced him to march out of the building and along the empty night streets until they got to a sports stadium, where he was brought inside. He stood in the dark open field, aware that there was now a sizable crowd of other men standing beside him in the still, inky night. Samir had no idea what the point of all this was until he suddenly heard shots ring out. To either side of him, bodies began to fall. Samir realized that he and the group were targeted for extermination.

Instinctively Samir fell down to the ground as if shot. He lay there in the darkness, as immobile as he could manage, hearing the voices of the militants as they walked around the arena. They finally left. Samir cautiously crawled toward an exit and, finding it locked, was able to pile up containers to create a makeshift ladder so he could climb over the fence and drop to the other side. He returned home to his family, and that very night he hustled his two wives and seven children out of the house. They found their way to the home of a relative who took them in for a few days, until they moved again to homes of other relatives and friends, living like nomads to escape the sight of the ISIS security guards.

Within a few weeks they could hear the noise of battle moving closer from the eastern side of the city. Mosul was close to being liberated from ISIS. So one night, when they thought that the time was ripe, the family fled the city, joining a stream of refugees like themselves who were carefully avoiding the main roads and their checkpoints—since they did not know whether the checkpoints would be manned by ISIS or opposition soldiers. Finally, after going through fields they found a checkpoint manned by the Kurdish Peshmerga, who brought them to a transition center. Within days, he said, they were assigned tents in the Hasan Sham refugee camp, where they have been ever since.

Their stories were remarkably similar to the many others that I heard in the several times that I came to this camp and others in Kurdistan in visits over several years. Most people I met were like Samir and Ahmad—ordinary folk who for a time accepted ISIS rule and its ideology for opportunistic reasons. Initially, at least, the ISIS movement was not a major disruption in their daily lives, until conditions got worse and the attitude of the ISIS command began to become more harsh. It was like "living in a prison," one woman told me. In general, now that they were in the camp they seemed relieved to be free of ISIS control.

There were a couple of exceptions, however. One was a woman, Hadiya. I was seldom able to speak with women since they were more hesitant about interacting with foreigners, though often I found that when they did begin to speak it was hard to stop them. Hadiya was no exception in this regard.

Hadiya's tent was a plastic partition in what had formerly been a long shed for chickens but now had been divided into fifty or so compartments approximately eight by twelve feet, most of them occupied by single women with children. Though the cinderblock walls and metal roof were more substantial than the camp tents, the thin plastic partitions did little to soften the noise. With the large number of children in the building there was a constant din.

Hadiya had four children, with ages varying from a few months old to five or six. She was not in ISIS, she said, though she admitted that her husband had been an ISIS soldier. She was a divorced woman with three children living in Mosul when she met him. He was an American citizen, she said, but a Muslim with Arabic-speaking ancestry, who came to Syria and then to Mosul to fight for ISIS. At that time he took up residence near where she was living and befriended her, and before long they were living together as husband and wife. She bore another child. He also had another wife, a Sudanese woman, with whom he stayed every other night.

When the siege to liberate Mosul began in 2016, her husband joined the fight to protect ISIS, though he would usually come home in the evenings to be with one of his wives. The next year, when the fighting was closer to the center of the city, her husband asked his ISIS commander whether he should stay and fight, and he was told that the situation was hopeless. If he wanted to survive, the commander told him, he should leave while he had the chance. So he took his two wives and children and slipped out of Mosul into Kurdistan. When they surrendered to the Peshmerga soldiers the husband was separated from his families, and they have not seen him since. He was put into a detention center for further investigation and a decision about whether or not to put him on trial. He has lived in this limbo state for over a year. Hadiya has received a communique, however, indicating that he is in good health and that he hopes to be reunited with his wives and children.

If ISIS came back and retook Mosul, I asked, would she go back to the city and live under ISIS rule again? She told me that she would go wherever her husband wanted to go. She professed no ideological allegiance, though she added that she was proud that her husband had fought against the Shi'a on behalf of the Sunni community. Like Samir and Ahmad, she saw the ISIS struggle against the Iraqi government in ethnic terms, a case where Sunni Arabs were standing up to their Shi'a oppressors.

Another fellow in the camp put the matter more directly. "With ISIS," he said, "you don't know whether they will kill you or not, but the Shi'a definitely will." For this man, Khalid, it was a matter of accepting the devil that you didn't know in preference to the one that you did. Khalid was in the detention area of the camp, separated from the rest of the refugees for further interrogation. He was under suspicion of being an ISIS operative, even though he professed his innocence. Still, I noticed that there were around a dozen men with him who clearly respected Khalid and regarded him as some sort of leader. He claimed to have been an English teacher at one time, and he spoke to me in broken English.

Khalid was in his early forties and had a hard, intense look about him. He seemed to be studying me, perhaps to figure out whether I was really the academic that I said I was or a spy or some other kind of government agent. Regardless of what assumptions he had made about me he was willing to talk, answering even my questions about ISIS, which he described as a local movement for Sunni Arab protection, and not an alien intervention.

At one point I asked him whether he thought ISIS was a political movement or a religious one. He hesitated before answering, and then began to laugh. He said something in Arabic to his colleagues and they laughed also. Finally he said that he didn't know, maybe it was both. Or maybe, he said, it was a political movement dressed up like a religion. I said I agreed with him on that and he smiled and gave me a high five.

The Movements for Sunni Empowerment

As these stories indicate, most of the people in the camps whom I met had a certain ambivalence about ISIS. On the one hand, it was brutal and repressive. On the other hand it gave Sunni Arabs recognition and roles to play in the economy and administration of the region. It was a movement of Sunni empowerment.

Though ISIS seemed to most Western observers to have come out of nowhere, its territorial claims were very specific: the Arab Sunni heartland of eastern Syria and western Iraq. Before the leaders of the movement shortened its name to "the Islamic State" (or "Caliphate") it called itself *al-Dawla al-Islamiya fi al-Iraq wa al-Sham*, an Arabic phrase that can be translated into English as "the Islamic State of Iraq and Greater Syria." The term *al-Sham*, or "greater Syria," includes the Sunni Arab heartland of the Middle East, the present nation-states of Syria, Lebanon, Jordan, and Israel. This is the region that the French call "the Levant," which is why its initials in English are sometimes given as ISIL rather than ISIS. It is also called "Da'ish" or "Daesh," a word based on the acronym for the Arabic name for the movement. By coincidence, in Arabic the term *daesh* also means something like the word for "bullies," and for that reason ISIS leaders are annoyed by its usage. Probably also for that reason, the term persists among those victimized by it.

Though it dramatically vaulted into global attention in its territorial conquests of 2014 and the brutal methods that accompanied them, the movement had been around for several years. Its origins date back to 2003, during the social unrest that developed in Iraq after the invasion and occupation by United States military and the coalition troops that supported it. At that time the overthrow of the Iraqi dictator Saddam Hussein was greeted by a certain degree of apprehension within al-Anbar province and other areas of western Iraq where Arab Sunni Muslim communities dominated.

When I went to Iraq soon after the invasion, I spoke with Sunni leaders from al-Anbar province who told me that they did not mourn the loss of Saddam Hussein. But they feared the loss of Sunni power.[2] Even though Saddam's rule was secular, it had favored his own minority Sunni community. In post-Saddam Iraq, the Shi'a majority in the rich river valleys stretching from Baghdad to Basra had begun to claim power and marginalize the Sunnis. For this reason any movement that promised power to Sunnis in the region was appealing.

The Sunni shining knight who appeared on the scene in 2004 was a militant jihadi from Jordan, Abu Musab al-Zarqawi. Born into a refugee Palestinian family, the young Zarqawi turned to a life of drugs and petty theft, but later underwent a conversion into a strict form of Islam influenced by the rigid moral codes of the Wahhabi Islam prominent in Saudi Arabia. Among other things, it allowed for beheading as an acceptable punishment for those who threatened the faith.

The movement Zarqawi created in Iraq was based on these teachings and on the longing of Sunnis in the western region of the country to be free of both American military occupation and Shi'a political domination. He named his movement "al-Qaeda in Iraq," hoping to receive support from the international organization headed by Osama bin Laden and Ayman a- Zawahiri, at that time hiding out in Pakistan after the United States invasion and occupation of Afghanistan. Relations between Zarqawi and bin Laden were never good, however, since Zarqawi insisted on his own priorities and his own leadership style. The al-Qaeda leaders were uncomfortable with Zarqawi's extreme anti-Shi'a stance, and his easy adoption of beheading as an intimidating tactic, which bin Laden and Zawahiri thought would alienate people from the movement.

The al-Qaeda leaders were right, and though Zarqawi's movement flourished for a time with support from young radical Arab Sunnis, especially after the United States destroyed the city of Fallujah in 2004, the Sunni tribal elders were increasingly wary of Zarqawi's authoritarian leadership and his rigid Islamic policies. In 2006 Zarqawi was killed by US military forces. The new head of al-Qaeda in Iraq was an Egyptian, Abu Ayyub al-Masri, who kept the name of al-Qaeda for the movement but announced that the organization would be creating an Islamic state in the region, headed by an Iraqi Caliph, Abu Omar al-Baghdadi. Al-Masri and al-Baghdadi were killed by a US military strike in 2010 and their movement turned to a man who took the name of the fallen al-Baghdadi, naming himself Abu Bakr al-Baghdadi. It is this Baghdadi who later proclaimed himself the Caliph of the Islamic State.

For a time, however, the predecessor organization, al-Qaeda in Iraq, was defeated. In 2007, under the leadership of General David Petraeus, US troops were withdrawn from the Sunni regions of western Iraq and local tribal militants were empowered to turn against al-Qaeda in Iraq, which eventually restored the region to traditional tribal and religious leadership control. The operation was dubbed the "Awakening."

This solution worked well while the United States was still the occupying force in Iraq, but when the US military withdrew its troops in 2011, the responsibility for maintaining the support of the Sunni tribal leaders fell on the shoulders of the newly elected Prime

Minister Nouri al-Maliki and his Shi'a-dominated government in Baghdad. Alas, al-Maliki abandoned the Arab Sunni leaders, choosing to shore up his political support largely from his own Shi'a base by using government funding and positions as payouts to his political supporters. Once again, the Arab Sunnis regarded themselves as alienated and disenfranchised.

This is where al-Baghdadi and his Islamic State came back into the picture. In neighboring Syria an uprising began in 2011, based in part on Sunni Arab dissatisfaction. As in Iraq, the Arab Sunnis in Syria also felt marginalized by a government that privileged a religious community other than their own. The Syrian leader, Bashar al-Assad, was an Alawite, a sect related to Shi'a Islam whose members were privileged under Assad's regime. Understandably, Sunnis demanded greater involvement in public life. This Syrian uprising gave Iraq's al-Baghdadi a nearby base of operations as his cadres infiltrated the resistance fighters and built their own jihadi army, eventually controlling large sections of Sunni Arab territory in eastern Syria. Their main competition in that battle-weary country was another movement affiliated with al-Qaeda, the al-Nusra Front, with which the al-Qaeda leader Ayman al-Zawahiri urged al-Baghdadi to collaborate. Al-Baghdadi was determined to go his own way, however, rejecting al-Nusra and the name "al-Qaeda," and proclaimed that his movement was now separate, and in fact was an Islamic State. In 2014 the movement gathered huge swaths of Syrian territory under its control and roared over the borders between Syria and Iraq, conquering Iraq's second largest city, Mosul, which it plundered for its wealth and military armament.

As my conversations in the refugee camps indicated, the Sunnis in the region who supported ISIS did so for largely opportunistic, not ideological, reasons. These Sunnis and their tribal leaders were seen as fair-weather friends by the ISIS leadership, which knew that they could easily turn against ISIS. After all, this is what had happened earlier during the Awakening, and al-Baghdadi must have remembered how his fickle Sunni followers had abandoned al Qaeda in Iraq at that time. For this reason he instituted a reign of terror in ISIS- controlled areas to intimidate his own Sunni populace into compliance.

It is fair to describe ISIS as a terrorist regime, since it used extreme acts of violence to control both its enemies and its own population. The horrific images of savage beheadings of Western journalists and aid workers that were posted on the Internet were matched by dozens, perhaps hundreds, of images of beheadings of recalcitrant Sunnis under ISIS's control who had refused to go along with its demands. Even worse was the ISIS treatment of the many other residents of the region who dared to identify as Christians, Yazidis, and other minorities—or even as modern people who liked to dress in a Western style. For ISIS, terror was an instrument of governance and social control.

But even terror can go only so far in controlling people against their will. So when cities such as Mosul were liberated, most of the population was relieved to see ISIS go. They were not, however, happy to see their homes destroyed, their cities obliterated. And they were not pleased to see a Shi'a government take charge, and to subject themselves to marauding bands of Shi'a militia.

One of the refugees with whom I spoke in the camps came from the western Iraqi city of Ramadi. Omar had fled from ISIS-controlled Ramadi only to flee again from the dangers of the Shi'a militia. Before ISIS had conquered the city he had worked for a time for the Iraqi government. When ISIS militia discovered this connection he was imprisoned, and he broke free only when the city was re-conquered by Iraqi forces and ISIS abandoned the city. Omar then went to Baghdad hoping to reestablish his life, since his home at Ramadi had been destroyed and he could not return there. But in Baghdad he found that his life was in danger from Shi'a militia. He said that the Shi'a treated all of the Sunnis from Western Iraq as if they were ISIS supporters. He eventually found his way north to Kurdistan, where the Kurds treated him much better than the Shi'a Arabs, and accepted him into a refugee camp.

Now Omar, like the others with whom I spoke, including Samir, Ahmad, Hadiya, and Khalid, was waiting. They could not go back to their homes since their cities had been destroyed. They feared the Shi'a militia and they also feared the return of ISIS. Already there were pockets of guerilla fighters in the villages. For that reason they could not go anywhere else. So they stayed in the camp, waiting.

Unrepentant Jihadi Warriors

Muhammad was brought to the warden's office to meet me. He was a tall stocky man in his late twenties, sporting a typical Arab beard. Though he had not talked with a foreigner before, he seemed to be assured by the warden's introduction that I was an acceptable person, and was in fact the academic that I claimed to be. The warden had cut through some red tape to allow me to meet with him and other prisoners, and provided a small conference room on one side of his office as the venue for our conversations.

I had come to this prison in Kurdistan to meet with true believers in the ISIS cause. I knew that the opportunistic attitude of Samir, Khalid, and many of the other people I met in the refugee camps, who had supported ISIS as a movement of Sunni empowerment, was only part of the story. I knew that there were others, the inner core of hardened ISIS militants, who were firm believers in the ISIS ideology of the Caliphate, and likely more resistant to change.

This prison was full of such people. Many were ISIS warriors who had been interrogated, tried, and sentenced to prison terms relatively recently after the fall of ISIS in Mosul. Others had been in prison for years, dating back to the days of al-Qaeda in Iraq in 2004. Muhammad was in both categories, since he had been in and out of the prison for over ten years. When the warden asked me what kind of prisoners I wanted to meet, I told him that I wanted to meet with those who still embraced the jihadi ideology, and also with those who had abandoned it, since I wanted to understand how terrorism ends.

Muhammad was just the person for the second category, the warden told me; he was one of those who had abandoned the ISIS cause. In fact, he was so much on the outs with the ISIS inner circle that he had to be separated from the rest of the prison population for his own safety. The warden seemed fond of him, and occasionally would invite him to his office for conversations. Muhammad seemed at home in the office, enjoying the tea and salty snacks that were provided. But as soon as we were alone in the conference room, just the two of us and my Kurdish colleague who served as an Arabic interpreter, his mood changed.

"I don't tell the warden everything," he told me in the middle of our conversation. "There are some things he will never understand."

What he was referring to was the apocalyptic ideology of the ISIS caliphate, in which Muhammad continued to be a firm believer. Where he had parted company with the ISIS movement was over its leadership, which he rejected. He observed infighting

and petty politics and blatant grabs for power among those immediately superior to him. The collapse of the territorial control of the
movement and the maintenance of a temporal caliphate was a disaster of military strategy, he said, for which he thought that the top
leadership was directly responsible. It was this organizational
opposition to the ISIS movement—not its ideology—that put him at
odds with the other former ISIS militants.

Muhammad had been fighting a jihadi struggle for most of his
life. He joined the movement that preceded ISIS, al-Qaeda in Iraq,
when he was only fifteen. He was raised in a Sunni Arab family that
was privileged during the Saddam regime. His father was an army
officer, and they enjoyed a comfortable middle-class family home
in Mosul. All of that came crashing down when the US military
removed Saddam's regime and the Shi'a were in control. His father
lost his job and the family was suddenly plunged into poverty.
Muhammad was thirteen at the time, and the memories of this
family tragedy were etched into his mind.

Two years later, when al-Qaeda in Iraq came recruiting,
Muhammad was ready to join. When I asked him why he joined the
movement, he looked puzzled, as if his family's situation was sufficient explanation. But then he gave other answers. He said he
was curious, and besides, all of his friends were doing it. He met
with some of the leaders and found them to be inspirational. At
age fifteen, with no other prospects for his future, he joined the
movement.

At first he saw the al-Qaeda movement primarily as a way of
restoring power and dignity to Sunni Arabs. Unlike the global mission of al-Qaeda led by Osama bin Laden, the Iraqi version was
stridently anti-Shi'a. Its ideology portrayed the Shi'a as agents of
the devil, and justified any kind of assault against them and those

that supported them. In Iraq after 2003, that meant the American military. Guerilla attacks against Americans, along with Shi'a religious and government establishments, were part of the movement's mission.

Muhammad served a variety of roles. The movement was very egalitarian, he said, in that they would rotate the duties of those who were involved with it. His job would be to help in transporting weapons, providing communications, and participating in fighting teams. In the early days, he said, there was a great sense of camaraderie among the militants and the sense that all were equal within the group.

Within two years, however, Muhammad was arrested. He was part of a team that was cornered and captured. Although there was no specific evidence of his committing crimes, he was culpable of being part of what was regarded as a terrorist organization. He was sent to a prison camp, Camp Bucca, in the extreme southern tip of Iraq near the city of Umm Qasr. The American military had taken over this detention facility when they occupied Iraq in 2003 and named it after Ronald Bucca, a New York City fire marshal who died in the collapse of the World Trade Center towers in the 9/11 attacks.

Muhammad loved being in prison. "The Americans were so stupid," Muhammad told me, "thinking that they would punish us by putting us all together into this facility with nothing else to do but to learn from one another." The camp was nicknamed "Jihadi University" by the militants of al-Qaeda in Iraq who were detained there. The inmates organized themselves into classes that were taught by the more experienced fighters. The subjects were Islamic theology, militant organization, and strategy.

It was in Camp Bucca, Muhammad told me, that his commitment to the movement changed. He became less concerned with anti-Shi'a support for Sunni Arab empowerment, and focused more on religion and the promised Caliphate. He increasingly saw his participation in the movement as one that was a requirement of his religious duty to live a strict and righteous life, and to punish those who were impediments to this rigid Islamic lifestyle. The prime impediments were the heretics, namely the Shi'a, and the invaders, their American enablers. Hence the goals of the movement were not changed, but his motives were transformed into those fitting a spiritual quest, and his battle became a cosmic war.

After two years Muhammad was released from prison. He was nineteen years old at the time and ready for new adventures, though by then the al-Qaeda movement was largely moribund. Zarqawi, the leader of al-Qaeda in Iraq, had been killed, and the Awakening movement designed by General Petraeus had armed traditional Sunni tribal leaders and their militia to turn against the jihadi movement.

Muhammad rejoined what remained of the movement, but found that it was rife with infighting. The old spirit of egalitarian camaraderie had vanished. He got into fights with some of the other militants, one of whom stabbed him in the stomach. Muhammad lifted up his shirt to show me the scars that he still bore from that experience. After that he retreated from active militancy. For a time Muhammad lived a relatively normal life. He got married and fathered a daughter and worked at odd jobs. But he was waiting, he said, for the opportunity to return to the struggle.

He soon had his chance. In 2011, when movements of democratic protest associated with the Arab Spring swept throughout the

Middle East and new opportunities for Sunni Arab militancy emerged in neighboring Syria, Muhammad was thrilled. In 2012 he crossed over the border to join the jihadi activists. At first he was associated with al-Nusra. Then in 2013 when an Iraqi activist who had been in al-Qaeda in Iraq started a new movement in Syria, Muhammad joined it. Muhammad admired the new leader, Abu Bakr al-Baghdadi. He cheered when his home city of Mosul was conquered by ISIS in 2014, and when al-Baghdadi mounted the pulpit of the central mosque in the city to proclaim himself as the Caliph of the Islamic State.

Muhammad returned to Iraq to work with the movement. He was still with ISIS, but increasingly he became unhappy with the local leaders with whom he had to deal on a regular basis. He said that he was loyal to al-Baghdadi as the Caliph, and admired the spokesperson for the movement, Abu Muhammad al-Adnani. But he found the local organization to be corrupt, self-serving, and ineffective. Though not formally resigning from the movement, he would just wander off from time to time and distance himself from it.

Paradoxically, it was during one of those times that he was again captured. He was in a grey area between ISIS and government territory when Iraqi soldiers identified him. His face was familiar, he said, since he had been associated with the movement for years. The trial and conviction came relatively quickly, and ever since he has been in the prison where I was meeting with him.

What about now, I asked Muhammad. If he had the opportunity would he join the movement again?

It depended, he said, on the leadership. He did not like violence, he said, and thought that at times the militants in the movement went too far. But the movement had no choice, he said, since the Shi'a oppressors were violent. So they had to respond in kind.

Muhammad said that he had had Shi'a friends in the past, also Christians and Yazidis. He had nothing against them personally. Even Americans, he said, looking at me. It all depends on the person.

But then he said that if the Islamic State was actually established, anyone within it had to live by its pure and rigid standards. They would have to convert or die. Christians were people of the book, they could buy their way out. But others, including Shi'a and Yazidi, would have to leave or die.

Even your old friends, I asked? Yes, he said, dispassionately. One hundred percent allegiance was the price to pay for participation in the Islamic State.

If he got out of prison tomorrow, he said, he would wait until the opportunity came to fight again, to join a movement that he thought was worthy of his support, a new Caliphate. Until then he would go home to his wife and daughter and work at an ordinary job, perhaps mechanical repair or carpentry. But some day, he said, the opportunity would come to fight again.

The stories of other jihadi militants with whom I spoke in prison were similar to Muhammad's. Several others also expressed dissatisfaction with the leadership, they said, which they thought had let them down. But like Muhammad, none showed remorse. And all seemed willing to fight again if the opportunity presented itself.

There were, however, varying degrees of support for the apocalyptic ideology that the Islamic State touted. Most focused on the grievances of Sunni Arabs under Shi'a control. One described the oppression of Shi'a as worse than the violence of Osama bin Laden. Some, like Muhammad, pledged loyalty to the Caliphate and saw that as the main mission of the movement. Others scarcely mentioned it. It was if the fall of the organizational power of ISIS also crushed its apocalyptic fervor.

One of the most religious prisoners I met was Rahim. In prison he served as an imam, leading the Friday evening worship. He also led classes on Islamic theology. Interestingly, however, when I talked with him about his involvement in the movement he spoke less about the Caliphate ideology of ISIS than the other old militant, Muhammad. His emphasis was on the oppression of Sunni Arabs under Shi'a control. When I asked him specifically about the revival of the Caliphate, a key feature of the ISIS ideology, he said somewhat hesitantly, "that's possible." For him the vision of great warfare had retreated to the realm of spiritual aspirations, rather than political goals.

Rahim said that he had not been all that religious as a young man. He was sixteen when the Saddam Hussein regime was toppled and life in Mosul began to radically change. It was then that he began to think about Islam, and what the difference was between Shi'a and Sunni. We are all Arabs, he said, though he was convinced that the sectarian differences led people into quite different attitudes about life and society. He came to the conclusion that Sunni Islam was more authentic and cohesive than Shi'ism, less selfish and aggressive. He began to regard Shi'a not just as heretics, but as dangerous enemies of true Islam.

Rahim began attending mosque more faithfully. There he met another young man his age whom he befriended. He was a jihadi militant, it turned out, and when the police came looking for him Rahim let him hide out in his house. The police discovered him, however, and hauled in Rahim as well. He was charged with harboring a criminal and sentenced to prison.

The prison he was sent to was the same Bucca camp where Muhammad was incarcerated and which was he had described as "Jihadi University." Rahim had a similar experience. He attended classes on Islamic theology and jihadi ideology. When he was released two years later he was a hardened and well-trained militant. He continued to work as a taxi driver, but also served as a messenger, carrying letters with him to different parts of Iraq where jihadi forces were at work.

It was on one of these taxi runs that Rahim was stopped. The Iraqi police found the letters and identified him as a former jihadi prisoner. He was immediately suspected of continuing to be part of the movement. Rahim was taken away for interrogation, and turned over to the US military for what they called "enhanced interrogation."

For weeks Rahim was detained and subjected to various kinds of torture, including sleep deprivation and beatings. The worst, he said, was waterboarding, since he thought that he was going to die. Eventually he confessed, he said, adding that everyone in the interrogation center did, simply to stop the torture. I asked him what crimes he confessed to, and he said he didn't remember. It didn't make any difference, he would have confessed to anything just to make them stop.

As a result of his confession he was given a long prison sentence, and he ended up in the prison where I met him. Rahim doesn't expect to be released soon. But if he is, he said that he would not live in Iraq any longer, as long as it was controlled by Shi'a. He would move to Egypt or Dubai, or anywhere else. But if the Islamic State movement was revived, that might make a difference, he said.

An Apocalyptic Cult

For Rahim, as for Muhammad, joining al-Qaeda and later the Islamic State was a transformative event. It was a part of their spiritual journey to find a more authentic form of Islam, and to clarify their own Sunni identity in the face of Shi'a oppression. In both cases they were recruited into the movement by more seasoned members. The process of recruitment, however, was not haphazard; it was a well-developed scheme.

Muhammad described the movement's design for recruiting new members. It was a process not unlike that of recruitment and initiation into a secret fraternity, or conversion into a religious cult. They would infiltrate into a group of young men, usually teenagers with no employment and no clear goals, and slowly bring them to the jihadi cause. It had three stages, Mohammad said, each characterized by an Arabic word beginning with the letter "t:" تسكن *tammaskan,* تمكن *tammakan,* and تفرعن *tafar'aan.* Each of these described a stage in the developing involvement of a young man targeted for recruitment into the jihadi movement.

The first T, *tammaskan,* means to "stick by" someone, to embrace him in an intimate friendship. Mohammad explained that they would usually target a young guy who might be flattered by the friendship of an active older man. The ISIS recruit would become his pal and only occasionally discuss religious and political matters.

The second T, *tammakan,* "control," referred to moment in which the recruiter would play a more dominant role. He would become more directive in telling the teenager where he had gone wrong in life and what to do about it. The conversation about religion and politics would become explicit, with the clear implication that the young man should learn from these lessons.

The third T, *tafar'aan,* means "act like a Pharoah," or enslaving. After it had become clear that the young man was responding to the authoritative relationship with the ISIS recruiter, he was ready to be made captive to the ISIS cause. In some cases there would be a kind of initiation, a recognition that the young man was now ready to take on a role in an important cause and become a servant in a secret circle of friendship.

Muhammad himself had gone through these stages of recruitment when he was a teenager in the town of Mosul. He described this strategy with no shame. In fact, he seemed proud of how effective it was, and how lucky his recruits were to join what he regarded as a sacred cause.

Another form of recruitment involved Muhammad sneaking into Sunni areas of cities at night and painting anti-government slogans on walls. When daylight came and the authorities saw the slogans they would send security forces to raid the district and arrest large numbers of young people, who of course had nothing to do with the slogan-painting. They would then be sent to prison, and it was there that they were vulnerable to jihadi workshops and messengers who would often convert them to the jihadi perspective. This tactic also had the effect of making their families angry at the government security forces and less likely to object to al-Qaeda or ISIS control.

Part of the lure of the recruitment was that it presented the inductees with an exciting and radically new view of the world. This was one in which great cosmic forces were at work. The movement into which they were invited was, they were told, at the leading edge of a cosmic battle. This confrontation was a clash between good and evil that would usher in the last days of the planet and signal the arrival of the Islamic savior, the Mahdi. Though only some of the fighters were propelled by this belief, at least Muhammad and some of the other Sunni Arabs in ISIS-controlled territory shared it. It was the dominant motif for the true believers of the movement.

This "ISIS apocalypse," as William McCants described it in a perceptive book with that title, is a kind of extreme variant of Wahhabi Muslim apocalyptic thinking.[3] Soon after the fiery leader of al-Qaeda in Iraq, Abu Musab al-Zarqawi, was killed in 2006, his successor, Abu Ayyad al-Masri, turned to apocalyptic thinking to characterize the movement as the Caliphate that would emerge at the end times. He thought that the Mahdi would be coming soon and that the faithful had to act quickly to establish a Caliphate to receive him. His successor and self-proclaimed Caliph of the Islamic State, Abu Bakr al-Baghdadi, shared that view. The name of the ISIS online magazine, *Dabiq*, referred to a town in northern Syria that was the location of the battle of Marj Dabiq between the Ottoman Empire and the Mamluk Sultanate in 1516. It was an ISIS belief that this town would be the location of the final battle between true believers and infidels that would usher in the apocalypse. For that reason, the ISIS leadership fought hard to retain control over the town, and when it fell to Syrian government forces in 2016 they renamed their magazine. The new name was *Rumiyah,* which also has apocalyptic significance, since the forces from Rumiyah (Rome, and by extension all of Europe and the West) would attack the Muslim forces and be defeated in the final apocalyptic battle.

The strict code of behavior and extreme brutality in dealing with perceived enemies are aspects of the ISIS movement that are grounded in some accounts of medieval Islamic history and practice. The relation between this kind of reign of terror and religion is problematic, however. One can claim that the ISIS policies are vicious because their religious understanding requires the faithful to act this way. More likely, however, their yearning for an intimidating form of extreme violence needed justification, which they found in ancient tradition. Either way it is an eerie relationship between religion and extreme violence.

Many have challenged whether ISIS should be called "Islamic". In the heyday of ISIS, Muslims around the world rose up to protest against what they described as the non-Muslim attitudes and actions of the movement. Iyad Ameen Madani, the Secretary General of the Organization of Islamic Cooperation, a group that represented fifty-seven countries and 1.4 billion Muslims, said ISIS "has nothing to do with Islam and its principles." Similar denunciations came from leading Muslim clergy in Egypt, Turkey, and around the world. Even in ISIS-controlled areas of Syria and Iraq, few of the traditional Muslim leaders supported the movement; ISIS would install its own imams.

Whether or not ISIS ideology is true to Islam is a matter of debate. There is no question, however, that leaders of ISIS claimed Muslim authority for their actions, strict shari'a law as the basis of their jurisprudence, and the promise of salvation for those recruited into its ranks. The credentials of al-Baghdadi gave some credibility to this religious appeal. He was a cleric whose family claimed ancestry to the family of the Prophet. He received a PhD in Islamic Studies from the Islamic University of Baghdad (not Baghdad University, as is sometimes misreported, which is a secular state institution). His thesis was on how to perform proper recitations of the Qur'an.

Though he was not a specialist in Quranic studies, per se, al-Baghdadi knew the scriptures and the tradition of Islam better than most jihadists. Osama bin Laden had no religious credentials, for example; though he pretended to be an engineer, his college training was in business management. Ayman al-Zawahiri was a medical doctor, and al-Baghdadi's predecessor in leading al-Qaeda in Iraq, Abu Musab al-Zarqawi, was a street thug from Jordan. By contrast, al-Baghdadi looked fairly legitimate. His credentials alone did not make the movement Islamic, however. Nor did the Islamic whitewashing of the regime's terrorist actions and cruel restrictions make them Muslim. The judgment is in the eye of the beholder. And to most Muslims, ISIS represented the antipathy of the faith. For the few, the true believers in ISIS's cosmic war, the movement constituted their whole world.

Once one has entered into this alternative world, is there any retreat from it? In my conversations, former ISIS militants frequently responded like the two that I earlier described, both of whom have altered their view of the immediacy of the cosmic war. Muhammad regarded it as a deferred hope. Rahim relegated it to the realm of spiritual aspiration. Neither quite abandoned the idea, but their reconsiderations significantly changed the way it affected their present-day actions.

Could the image of apocalyptic struggle be abandoned completely? This is in part the goal of some of the counterterrorism projects aimed at former militants. An American psychiatrist has interviewed dozens of former ISIS activists with the intention of finding those who would recant on film and thus create counterterrorism videos.[4] She hoped these would persuade jihadi-minded viewers that they should be wary of the ISIS ideology and abandon it if they have already accepted it. Most of the activists who were willing to be in her videos and testify that they have completely rejected ISIS and its ideology, however, were not deeply involved in the movement in the first place. Those who were showed some remorse for its failures but in general most of them, like several I met in an Iraqi prison, continued to believe to some extent in the idea of a Caliphate and many endorsed the legitimacy of fighting in the future for an Islamic State. Others were vague and noncommittal and clearly attempted to avoid anything that might further incriminate them. Many denied any involvement with the movement.

One account involved an "ISIS emir" who was in prison in Kurdistan.[5] He was originally from Kirkuk and had studied shari'a law. He gradually turned towards the ideology of the Islamic State by reading the book *Kitab at-Tawhid* (*The Book of Divine Unity*) by the eighteenth-century Saudi founder of the Wahhabi form of extreme Islam, Muhammad ibn Abd al-Wahhab. The emir turned towards the Islamic State movement after seeing their videos on YouTube that showed it following strict shari'a tenets, including cutting off the hands of thieves and throwing suspected homosexuals off of tall buildings. "They were really living it," he said. In his case an acceptance of the militant Wahhabi ideology came before he joined the movement, so he did not need additional theological training. In fact he was immediately put in charge of training sessions in Islamic theology. The emir defended the military practices of ISIS, including suicide bombings, even by children, whom he claimed all volunteered to go as martyrs. (The movement regarded any boy old enough to ejaculate to be an adult man, and therefore allowed even thirteen-year old boys to carry out attacks.) They were eager to go, he said. And he approved of the beheadings of heretics, since that was prescribed in some Islamic legal codes.

But when he was shown videos of burning people alive and Yazidi women who had been taken as sex slaves, he seemed somewhat remorseful. "We made mistakes," he admitted. But that was the closest he came to a show of regret.

The Global Jihadi Movement

"Fighting for the Caliphate is the most glorious duty a Muslim can undertake," wrote one ISIS militant. This statement of faith in the ideology of cosmic war did not come from a Sunni Arab in Iraq or Syria, however. It was uttered in a Twitter account by a young Canadian who had taken up the cause and moved to Syria to fight in the struggle. On Twitter he was able to profess his faith to his friends back home and to the online jihadi community that he now regarded as family.

One of the striking features of the ISIS organization is that a sizable number, perhaps 30,000 or more, were fighters from outside the region. They were lured into the struggle through an aggressive and sophisticated online recruitment effort involving Twitter and other social media; YouTube videos; a sleek online magazine in English, Arabic, and other languages; and chat rooms and websites, some of them on the dark web in encrypted sites that could not easily be traced or removed.

Al-Baghdadi's strategy of recruiting young people from around the world to participate in a glorious struggle succeeded perhaps far beyond his expectations. For them the image of cosmic war was universal, engaging would-be soldiers from far corners of the globe. Initially I was puzzled over this strategy. It seemed to me that it would be a handicap from a military perspective to have to endure young fighters from many places who had no army training.

Many of them knew virtually no Arabic and were often ignorant of even the basic tenets of Islam. Some were more obviously useful, however; the volunteers who came from Libya and other Arabic-speaking regions could be used in regular military encounters. "They are all foreigners," one refugee told me in describing the ISIS soldiers who captured his village in northern Iraq, saying that although they spoke a kind of Arabic he didn't recognize the accent. In this case it showed that Arabic-speaking foreign fighters could be useful, but what about the English speakers from Canada and the United States, and the European residents? Of what use were they?

When I looked more closely at the careers of some of these foreign fighters I discovered the answer. The bulk of the suicide attacks that made ISIS so effective as a conquering force were carried out by young boys—the Caliphate Cubs—or non-Arabic speaking foreigners. To be a suicide bomber you didn't need to know Arabic or the finer points of Islamic theology. All you needed to do was to strap on an explosive belt and know when to ignite it. The blond, blue-eyed German twins, Kevin and Mark, who came from a town near Dortmund to fight for the Caliphate in Syria and Iraq, were in this category. They were there only a few months before they were called into suicide missions. Their deaths were proclaimed as martyrdoms and they were briefly featured in the online ISIS magazine, *Dabiq*.[6] Other foreigners served as guards and executioners, such as the notorious butcher featured in many online videos of beheadings, "Jihadi John." He was eventually identified as a resident of London, though for a time a British rap star who joined the movement was thought to be the culprit, in part because he posed with a severed head from an execution.[7]

Other foreign recruits did not need to journey all the way to Syria and Iraq to carry out their mission for the Caliphate. They were used as part of the ISIS strategy for globalizing their struggle. Often they were young members of expatriate Muslim communities in the United States and Europe who found themselves at sea in those secular cultures. The ISIS-related terrorists in the 2015 attack in San Bernardino, California, who killed fifteen and wounded twenty-two others, were American residents from Saudi Arabia. The Paris nightclub assault that year and the Brussels airport bombing in 2016 were carried out by Belgians of Moroccan descent. The Orlando shooter at a gay nightclub in 2016 was an American of Afghan descent; the attackers at the Istanbul airport that same year were from Kyrgyzstan, Uzbekistan, and Dagestan. Although all of these militants claimed loyalty to al-Baghdadi and his Caliphate, none were Syrian or Iraqi, the areas where ISIS had its territorial base. They were part of a global Caliphate army.

Those lured to this network came with a variety of motives. From an analysis of the Twitter and other online chatter, and from the evidence of the slick ISIS magazines aimed at an English-speaking global audience, one motivation appears to be primary: the desire to be involved in a great war. It was the same dramatic vision of apocalyptic cosmic war that animated the inner circle of the movement. For some of those attracted to this cosmic struggle it was an adventure, an opportunity to play out their computer-game fantasies of warcraft, valor, and gore. But for others this idea of cosmic war came out of their devotion to Islamic history and piety, and was accompanied with a conviction that they were laying their lives on the line for something of transcendent importance for Islamic civilization.

Motives for joining a movement such as ISIS can be complicated. Though religion and ideology may have been part of the equation there were social factors as well. Some of the young volunteers joined the movement to gain a sense of identity and to be a part of a community. For young people of Middle Eastern parentage who were living in Britain, Europe, and the United States, their experience of being in an alienated and marginalized group was overcome by the acceptance offered by ISIS. Initially their main form of participation was through online chat rooms and Twitter feeds.

My own student research assistants have monitored these Twitter accounts and found that the conversation was dominated by a sense of the importance of the cause, and the sharp we-they distinction between members of the movement's community and all outsiders, whether or not they were Muslim. A Canadian research scholar, Amarnath Amarasingam, who has interacted with many young Canadian volunteers on Twitter, concurs that community is an important part of the appeal. Many of the Twitter users called themselves members of the Baqiyah family, using the Arabic term for "enduring" that ISIS employed as one of its hallmarks.

"Trust me, I've never felt like I've belonged anywhere until I met the brothers and sisters online," one young volunteer told Amarasingam. "The Internet keeps us connected, keeps us a family," he added. Then Amarasingam asked the young man to say more about the sense of belonging he felt in the Baqiyah family, and he responded that he felt more authentic as a person within the Internet community: "sometimes it's like the person on line is the real you."[8]

Since this community exists in cyberspace rather than geographic territory it is hard to determine when someone leaves it or abandons the notion of cosmic war. My assistants monitoring the chat sites confirmed that the sites continued to be active, even after the last piece of ISIS-held territory was captured in March 2019, and after the killing of the Caliph, al-Baghdadi, later that year. In fact, as soon as the news of al-Baghdadi's death was confirmed and a new Caliph was anointed, many in the online community were eager to proclaim their loyalty to the new Caliph.

But many were not. How many is hard to determine, since few announced their dissatisfaction with the movement online, or declared that they were no longer true believers. A rare example was recorded from a Twitter feed where one follower said that the Caliphate was "a disgrace," but it "imbued in us a renewed sense of hope and longing."[9] Like Muhammad, the jihadi fighter with whom I spoke in prison, he was disenchanted with the ISIS organization, blaming it for its failure, but still clinging to the idea of a Caliphate.

Others registered their unhappiness and loss of faith in the movement silently, just by dropping out of sight online. My best estimate is that the online community declined perhaps twenty to forty percent in the months after 2018. By 2021 the numbers had dwindled even further. But that number is hard to determine since social media accounts are closed almost as quickly as they are opened and much of the communication has shifted to the encrypted dark web where it cannot be traced. It is also more difficult for marginal members to find access to it. So there is no question that the worldwide circle of those committed to the cosmic war of ISIS has diminished since its heyday, though it is difficult to say how many or why.

One way of understanding how some of these foreigners have changed their attitude towards the struggle is to follow the statements of those who have fled or been captured and released during the last stages of ISIS control. Scores of young people have now returned to their homes, and though many are silent and perhaps secretly believers in the Caliphate, others have shown remorse. A woman from Tunisia who had fled Raqqa with her children in the last days of ISIS control said that "if the Islamic State was real, I would not have left it," adding that she "would prefer to have died there than leave it." Instead, she said, it turned out to be "a band of vicious men intent on collecting cars and women."[10]

A German convert to Islam, Lucas Glass, who came to Syria to join ISIS when he was nineteen, said that most of the time that he served as a soldier, usually patrolling border areas, he was happy to be part of what he thought was a great effort to create an Islamic state. When he found out about the beheadings and other atrocities, he said, he wanted to leave but the ISIS commanders would not let him. In the final battles for ISIS territory Lucas was able to escape with his wife, but then was immediately put into detention in Syria. The German government will not accept him or any other ISIS member back into the country. Lucas is bitter about his experience, saying that "I got cheated," adding that "All of us got cheated, all of these foreigners, thousands of Muslims who came to join ISIS, got cheated."[11]

One of the best known spokespersons for ISIS, Muhammad Khalifa, was a Canadian who went by the *nom de guerre* Abu Ridwan. He is now languishing in a prison in Syria, but he would like to return to his home in Canada. The Canadian Khalifa had a promising technology career when he left to join the Islamic State, in which his English language skills enabled him to be the voice of many propaganda films, including the infamous *Flames of War,* that depicts beheadings and killings of prisoners. Khalifa himself is thought to be one of the masked executioners, though he has denied it. He would like to be released from prison, but not stay in Syria, which he regards as a dangerous place for himself, his wife, and his three children. For that reason he wants to return to Canada, but he is not willing to do so if he would be tried for war crimes. Moreover, he says that he has not lost faith in the idea of a Caliphate or the basic ideology of ISIS. He was happy to live in an Islamic State, he said, and would willingly return if one were to be established again.[12] But for now, he admitted, the struggle was over.

Another prominent ISIS figure from Canada, known in ISIS circles as Abu Huzaifa al-Kanadi, managed to escape Syria and slip back into Canada. He is now under the watchful eye of the Canadian intelligence agencies, and voluntarily undergoing a deradicalization program involving contact with moderate imams who are supposed to wean him into a nonviolent version of Islam. Though he seems to be compliant, there is no indication that he has really been converted. According to Amarasingam, who has interviewed over fifty returned ISIS fighters and their families, it is difficult to determine the returnees' inner thoughts. Many will say anything to deflect attention from them and allow them to return to ordinary society. "When do you say 'OK, he's probably not a threat anymore?'" Amarasingam asked, following with another rhetorical question, "At what point can you say that safely?" He admitted that "These are, I think, not easy questions."[13]

There are some accounts of former ISIS followers dramatically changing course. The *Los Angeles Times* featured a front-page story about Imran Rabbani, who was a seventeen-year-old New Yorker from a Pakistani Muslim immigrant family when he was lured into ISIS circles through his association with an older friend.[14] Unknown to Imran, his communications with the friend were bugged by the

FBI and eventually they were arrested on charges of planning a terrorist attack on Times Square in New York City. Imran was sent to a detention center where the staff was trained to deal with former radicals. The staff members, including Muslim staff, treated them with respect and provided them with reading material about the psychology of brainwashing. When Imran was released from prison fourteen months later he was a changed man. He saw his ISIS flirtation as a horrible mistake, and began classes at New York University in preparation for going to law school.

The jury is still out, however, regarding just how effective deradicalization programs can be. A Nigerian author who has interviewed former members of the Boko Haram has his doubts. In an article that focuses on one Boko Haram member who went through an elaborate European-Union funded deradicalization program, the former terrorist admitted that Boko Haram had committed violent excesses and for that reason would not rejoin the movement, but he still "remained firm in his core beliefs."[15] Some of his friends also raised questions about the movement's tactics but then rejoined when the opportunity presented itself, in part because they had no job or income and were living on the streets. Others who were less committed to the cause were able to quietly rejoin society and put their radical pasts behind.

This conclusion is similar to my own observation of former ISIS fighters. For those who were involved at the periphery, such as the many foreign youngsters on online chat rooms and those whom I met in refugee camps who became tired of the hypocrisy and infighting within the movement, the videos of former ISIS participants denouncing the movement as corrupt ring true. They do not need much persuasion. Some of the true believers in the Caliphate and the cosmic war of the final apocalypse appear to have recanted, though their confessions are not always found to be believable. Others, like many of those former fighters I met in a Kurdistan prison, agree that the movement's organization was flawed, but they still harbor notions of the great Islamic Caliphate and yearn someday to become a part of the glorious war that will signal its coming. When that will happen is unknown. But they are willing to wait.

3   *The Militant Struggle of Mindanao Muslims*

"It took months for me to accept the idea that the government was no longer the enemy," the former general told me. Butch Malang had been commander of the guerrilla forces of the Moro Islamic Liberation Front during some of its most active years battling against the government. But then, he said, the political leaders of his movement began to enter into negotiations. He reluctantly agreed.[1]

We were meeting in a locale that seemed far from the guerrilla jungle enclaves that for decades had been Malang's hideouts. We were chatting in the garden of Notre Dame University, a Catholic university with a largely Muslim student body, which was the main institution of higher education in Cotabato City, in the heart of the Southern Philippine province of Mindanao. Malang was not dressed in military uniform, but his lined face bore the signs of decades of struggle.

Initially he could not accept the idea of negotiating with the enemy, the former commander told me. He had trouble sleeping at night. He lay awake wondering if they had made the right decision. He was concerned about the movement and the cause for which they had struggled. He was also concerned about himself, his own future, and whether he should support the political leaders or not.

Some of the other commanders of the movement chose not to. They refused to go along with the peace negotiations. One was the leader of a branch of the armed wing of the MILF, the Bangsamoro Islamic Armed Forces, led by Ameril Umbra Kato, When he rejected the peace negotiations in 2010, Kato gave his new militia a similar sounding name, the Bangsamoro Islamic Freedom Fighters. Its supporters still have not reconciled themselves to the peace process. Nor have the followers of Abu Sayyaf, another extremist faction of Moro independence movement fighters.

But for Butch Malang, the end was in sight. He accepted the idea that negotiations work, and joined the government-sponsored Coordinating Committee on the Cessation of Hostilities, for which he was appointed co-chair, representing the Moro Islamic Liberation Front. "My thinking now is on peace," he told me.[2]

The Long Struggle for Moro Recognition

It has taken a long time for some of the members of the movement to come to the point where peace is a real option. The Moro movement has been around for quite a while.[3] Although most of the Philippines is Christian, the southern region of Mindanao and the Sulu archipelago of islands stretching towards Indonesia and Malaysia have been Muslim for centuries. There were Muslim Sultanates on Mindanao prior to the Spanish conquest of the Philippines in the sixteenth century. In 1457 a sultanate was established that maintained its independence even during most of the colonial period. It was the Spanish who called the Muslims "Moros," thinking they were much like the Moors of Spain. After centuries of resistance the Sultanate of Sulu acknowledged Spanish authority at the end of the nineteenth century.

The spirit of independence continued, however, even after the Spanish-American War in 1898, after which the Philippines became a colony of the United States. The United States' attempt to pacify the Mindanao region by importing Christian settlers from other parts of the Philippines has led to a diverse population in the region. But it also intensified the passion for the native Muslims to have an independent Moro geographical and political identity. When Mindanao was seized by Japanese forces during World War II, the Moros waged a war of insurgency against the Japanese.

When the war ended and the United States granted the Philippines independence in 1946, the movement for an autonomous Muslim region in Mindanao took on a new life, partially in response to the policies of the newly independent Philippine leaders to integrate the area with the rest of the country. The former US policy of importing Christian Filipinos into the region as settlers was expanded by the new Filipino leaders, including Manuel Quezon, Ramon Magsaysay, and Ferdinand Marcos. Several fledgling Muslim movements emerged in reaction, including the Bangsamoro Liberation Organization (Bangsamoro means "the nation of Muslims") and the Muslim Independence Movement. Public protests were held throughout the area.

These movements grew over the years, and in 1972 President Marcos instituted martial law in the region in an attempt to quell the unrest. The result was the opposite. A strong new protest movement emerged that year, called the Moro National Liberation Front (MNLF). It brought together the most active members of the Bangsamoro Liberation Organization and the Muslim Independence Movement.

The MNLF carried out a campaign of public protests and clandestine insurgency strikes through its own paramilitary forces, hoping to secure government concessions. In 1976 leaders of the movement traveled to Libya, where Muammar Qaddafi hosted a negotiating meeting with representatives from the Philippines government. The agreement that was signed on that occasion promised an autonomous Muslim regional government.

The Tripoli Agreement was a double disaster. President Marcos did not fulfill all of its promises, and the MNLF insurgencies were revived. Moreover, its compromises so angered some of the MNLF leaders who were not included in the negotiations that they created a splinter organization of more determined Moro militants. This splinter movement was the Moro Islamic Liberation Front (MILF), led by the former MNLF commander Ustadz Salamat Hashim. Now the Philippine government was facing two groups of Moro militants, the MNLF and the even more violent MILF.

The violence continued into the 1980s. In 1986, President Corazon Aquino revived negotiations with the MNLF, this time meeting in Jeddah, Saudi Arabia. The result of these negotiations was the establishment in 1989 of the Autonomous Region of Muslim Mindanao (ARMM). It included only four provinces and few financial or political incentives were provided for the new autonomous region. Its creation marked a new mission for the MNLF, away from guerilla activities and into developing the governmental structure of the new ARMM entity. Though it gave the appearance of peace to the region, it was staunchly resisted by the MILF, which had already split from the MNLF over the Tripoli Agreement some ten years earlier. To the MILF leaders the tepid Jeddah peace agreement was the final act of the MNLF's capitulation to the government's attempt to coopt the movement.

But the MILF was not the only problem for the success of the new ARMM regional entity and the MNLF that had created it.

There were rumblings from within the MNLF itself. The movement was based in the Sulu peninsula, an arm of Mindanao that swept out towards Indonesia, and there a radical splinter group broke off from the MNLF in protest. This new movement, led by Abdurajik Abubakar Janjalani, adamantly opposed the peace agreement and was determined to continue the armed struggle against the Philippine government. It was called Abu Sayyaf ("the father of the sword").

Janjalani, the founder of Abu Sayyaf, had been a teacher of Islamic theology in the Sulu peninsula region of Basilan. He had studied abroad in Libya, Syria, and Saudi Arabia, and in the 1980s went to Afghanistan to join the mujahidin, the Muslim militia that was fighting against the Soviet Union. He was said to have met Osama bin Laden at the time, and to have received funding from him to help the radical Muslim struggle in Mindanao. Whether or not that was the case, he likely received Saudi money to help break from the MNLF and create his own movement. The Saudi money came from Muhammad Jamal Khalifa, a Saudi Arabian citizen who was posted in the Philippines as head of the International Islamic Relief Organization. A defector from the organization claimed that most of the funds were used for creating Wahhabi mosques and schools in the Sulu peninsula, but the funds also supported the activities of the Abu Sayyaf.[4]

Abu Sayyaf was formally inaugurated in 1991. This began a reign of terror that has characterized the movement up to the present, though the number of fighters peaked in the year 2000 at perhaps about one thousand. Its strategy has changed over the years. Initially it targeted only governmental outposts, but then broadened its attacks to include public buildings and transport, including the bombing of Superferry 14 in 2004. The boat was transporting passengers from the northern Mindanao city of Cagayan de Oro, and when it reached Manila Bay a bomb was ignited in one of the lower decks. 116 passengers, including a number of schoolchildren, were killed in the blast. Increasingly in the twenty-first century the movement has turned towards kidnappings and demands for ransom to secure the victims' release. This shameful practice turned out to be highly lucrative, earning the movement millions of dollars.

At the same time that the Abu Sayyaf was militantly active on the Sulu peninsula, the MILF was undertaking its own guerrilla operations against the government on the mainland of Mindanao. While most of the MNLF forces, aside from Abu Sayyaf, were quieted by the peace deal, the MILF forces accelerated their attacks. In 1996, however, a new president, Fidel Ramos, began negotiating with the MILF for a revised peace agreement that they might accept, one that eventually led to the replacement of ARMM with the Bangsamoro Autonomous Region of Muslim Mindanao that was established in 2019.

The Fighter Who Negotiated for Peace

"It was a long road to peace," I was told by one of the leaders of the Moro movement who was involved with the peace settlement.[5] I first met the young lawyer, Naguib Sinarimbo, a MILF strategist and negotiator, in the offices of the UN Development Program in Cotabato City several years before the agreement was finally signed in 2019. At the time he was an advisor on the Moro peace process. Sinarimbo was clean-cut, wearing dark-rimmed glasses and a V-neck sweater, and spoke articulately about the history and goals of the movement. Rather than looking like a Muslim militant, he appeared more like a young lawyer and bureaucrat, though he was both, a fighter and an attorney. He told me stories about how in his previous position with the government he became annoyed on work-related trips to Manila when co-workers in the government did not realize that he was Muslim. He would listen, quietly angry, as they denigrated the Moros and their political goals. That made him determined to fight even harder for the goals of the movement.

In my subsequent visits to the region I increasingly gained his confidence, and Sinarimbo told me how his political career developed. He first became politically active in college, he said, when he was a student at Mindanao State University in Marawi in the early 1990s. The campus was buzzing with radical talk about Muslim activism, not only in Mindanao but around the world. During this time a recruiter for the Bosnian conflict came to campus and Sinarimbo felt the call to join the movement and defend his Muslim brethren in this distant battle in the Balkans. He packed up, determined to join the struggle, but at the designated time when he was to travel, the recruiter didn't show up. Somewhat disappointed, Sinarimbo returned to his studies at Marawi.

It was after this experience that he realized that the struggle in which he should be engaged was not the distant battle of Muslims in former Yugoslavia, but at home in Mindanao. Increasingly he felt called to join the struggle for an autonomous Muslim Moro region.

One of the attractions was the camaraderie of his fellow activists, he said, for whom the cause was a life and death struggle. In his early days in the movement, he said that he took a pledge to die on behalf of movement. He saw himself as a soldier in a righteous war, in a cosmic conflict of absolute right versus absolute wrong, against an enemy who needed to be countered at any cost.

At first he participated in meetings of the Moro National Liberation Front, but became disenchanted with their moderate positions. Increasingly he was attracted to their rival organization, the Moro Islamic Liberation Front, a separatist movement that appeared to him to be tough and uncompromising. It was militant and specifically religious in its ideology. He said that when he joined it he felt that he was fighting for his faith, his community, his family, and himself.

I asked him why he preferred the MILF over the MNLF, and he explained that it was partly a matter of ideology, but also of ethnicity and location. The MNLF was based in the Sulu archipelago, and the leaders tended to speak the Visayan language; the MILF was based in West-Central Mindanao, where people in the Cotabato City vicinity spoke Maguindanao. For Naguib Sinarimbo, the MILF was the dominant movement in his home region, and the fellow fighters were his neighbors.

But there were also religious reasons that made it appealing, and nationalist ones. Sinarimbo thought that the MILF took a stronger stand for Moro rights and did not as easily capitulate to the government's demands. It was able to do this, in part, because of its insistence that Muslim identity and culture were at the core of the Moro demands, and in part because the movement had stronger leadership, Sinarimbo felt, than did the MNLF. Like many of his fellow activists, Sinarimbo thought that the MNLF's agreement with the Philippines government to create a new Autonomous Region In Muslim Mindanao (ARMM) was flawed. Though it had sounded like an effective resolution to the conflict, ARMM was in fact a fairly ineffective administrative demarcation without much power, and with very little economic impact. Sinarimbo, thought that the MNLF's deal was a sell-out that did little to provide political identity to the Moros or substantive economic and structural changes that would improve their lives.

Sinarimbo's group, the Moro Islamic Liberation Front, was self-consciously Muslim. It was founded by Hashim Salamat, whose name was often accompanied by the honorific "Ustadz," a religious teacher. He had studied at the premier Muslim educational institution in Cairo, Al Azhar University, where he was influenced by Egypt's Muslim Brotherhood. He adopted some of the Brotherhood's staunch religious stand and its image of godly warfare. Salamat believed that Muslim principles, including a ban on alcohol and tobacco, should be requisite for an autonomous Muslim state. He and the MILF movement rejected the ARMM negotiation between the MNLF and Philippine officials, and he proclaimed a jihad against the government. The movement collaborated on several military campaigns against the government with Abu Sayyaf during the earlier, more idealistic stages of the Abu Sayyaf movement, before it turned to kidnappings and pledged its support to ISIS. Though never as extreme as Abu Sayyaf, the MILF also engaged In violent encounters. Its supporters justified their acts with religion, and at times thought of themselves as engaged in divine warfare for a righteous cause.

As the years went by and a new century emerged, Sinarimbo, along with many of his MILF colleagues, realized that the movement's struggle was at a stalemate. The sporadic attacks of guerrilla warfare were not producing any tangible results. This sense of the realistic limits of their strategy led to gradual erosion of the absolutism of cosmic war. In time they became more conciliatory even as their rival, Abu Sayyaf, became more violent. The MILF entered into its own negotiations with the Philippine government for a comprehensive peace settlement that would create Bangsamoro—a

Moro State—in the Mindanao region to replace ARMM. As a lawyer familiar with the legal issues relating to a peace settlement, Sinarimbo became deeply involved in the negotiation process.

One of the significant features of the negotiated deal was an elaborate sharing of government funds raised from taxes and sales of natural resources. Another was a separate political structure that would allow for local Muslim-led political parties to become leaders in the legislature of the autonomous Muslim state. In 2014, the Bangsamoro agreement was signed, with high hopes that the new entity would bring the region the identity and tranquility which the movement had sought over many years.

There was a hitch, however. Before being implemented, the Philippines Congress had to pass a law enacting the provisions of the agreement. At a critical moment, a nasty encounter between Moro and government forces occurred. Before the bill was slated to be approved, an armed clash between the Philippines National Police and militia units related to the MILF at the village of Mamasapano in Mindanao resulted in over sixty deaths. Investigations after the incident blamed poor communications between the police and officials in the MILF for the confusion that led to the clash, but the public blamed the Moros. The time was not ripe for Congressional approval and 2015 ended without a vote on the issue.

In 2016, the Philippines elected a new president, Rodrigo Duterte, a colorful politician from the Mindanao city of Davao. When I was in Manila soon afterwards, I talked with staff members of the Presidential advisory office that monitors the peace process, and they were optimistic. One of the directors told me that Duterte had pledged to bring the Bangsamoro implementation bill up for a vote, though not until some revisions were made. The director suggested that maybe next year the agreement would finally be implemented, and she showed me a chart indicating June 2017, as the date for formal approval.[6] Other political observers were more skeptical. For the MILF cadres, even a year meant more waiting and frustration.

"I give the government two years at most," Naguib Sinarimbo told me.[7] He explained that the young members of the movement were impatient and wary of the compromises that the movement had already had to make. If the agreement were to be watered down further, or delayed for an indefinite period of time, their restlessness might lead to renewed militant action. Moreover, the credibility of the MILF leadership would be undermined and negotiations with the government would be mistrusted. The situation would be fertile for violence.

Reining in the Extremists

One of the persons most concerned about the renewal of military confrontation from elements of the MILF was the area commander Butch Malang, whom I mentioned at the beginning of this chapter. Though he had led his Moro fighters on a number of campaigns against the government in the past, Malang had renounced violence in favor of the 2014 peace agreement, and on my first meeting with him he was serving as Vice Chair of the MILF panel on the Coordinating Committee for the Cessation of Hostilities, a joint government-Moro movement organization that was charged with overseeing the demilitarization of the Moro militias and coordinating between the police and the movement to keep incidents such as the bloody encounter at Mamasapano from occurring.

Butch Malang knew his fighters, he told me, and he knew that the younger ones especially would be easily lured into more violent organizations than MILF if they were frustrated.[8] One such group, the Bangsamoro Islamic Freedom Fighters (BIFF), had already been involved, along with MILF militia, in the Mamasapano incident, and were ready to mobilize and attract new recruits as soon as the peace agreement seemed to be faltering. They were flirting with ISIS, he said, and he knew of several other small radical Moro gangs that were poised to become ISIS-affiliated as well. The continued failure to implement the peace agreement would be the trigger for them to expand and become publicly more violent.

This assessment was supported by Major Carlos Sol, a former Philippines army officer who was appointed director of the Coordinating Committee for the Cessation of Hostilities. Major Sol was raised in central Mindanao, and though he was Christian he knew the players in the Muslim movements well. When I talked with him about the situation in his map-lined office in Cotabato City, Major Sol explained some of the movements' internal politics.[9] He said that there were three other small groups of Moro fighters beside Abu Sayyaf that had pledged their support to ISIS. One, created by the nephew of the founder of BIFF, called itself ISIS of Mindanao.

As I mentioned earlier, Abu Sayyaf, which began as a faction of the Moro National Liberation Front, over the years had degenerated into a brigand gang that extracted money through extortion by taking hostages.[10] Estimates of their profits in recent years have ranged from twenty to thirty million dollars. When they kidnapped two Canadians, a Norwegian, and a Filipino woman at a resort in Samal Island in Mindanao in 2015, they initially demanded twenty-eight million dollars in ransom to free each of the foreigners; the Filipino woman was released. The Canadian government refused to pay the ransom money. Later Abu Sayyaf lowered the amount to eight million dollars each, but again the Canadian position was not to negotiate with terrorists. Abu Sayyaf responded by beheading both of the Canadians, which prompted the Norwegian government to begin negotiations for the release of the remaining hostage. He was eventually freed. It is not clear how much money was involved in his successful release.

In the twenty-first century, then, Abu Sayyaf has departed from the religious and nationalist goals that were the vision of its founder, Abdurajik Abubakar Janjalani, and his younger brother, Kadaffy Janjalani, who succeeded him when the founder was killed in a government clash in 1998. Khadaffy himself was killed eight years later, and in 2006 Isnilon Totoni Hapilon became the leader. Hapilon professed to be following the religious goals of his predecessors even though increasingly the movement gave the appearance of being a criminal gang.

It was Hapilon that turned the movement towards kidnapping and ransom demands, though he claimed to still be motivated by religious ideology. He found a convenient cover for his violent religious approach in the rhetoric of ISIS. In 2014, he pledged allegiance to Abu Bakr al-Baghdadi, and proclaimed the Abu Sayyaf to be in partnership with ISIS. He embraced the ISIS notion of apocalyptic cosmic warfare, and this notion was beneficial in justifying some of the more questionable aspects of the movement's behavior. Hapilon regarded cosmic warfare as something that would give religious credibility to the movement's use of beheadings, and, like ISIS, its justification for taking women captive as sex slaves, claimed to be temporary "wives." By 2020 there were only a few hundred militants remaining in the movement on the Sulu peninsula, though they were tacitly supported by villagers near the areas where the Abu Sayyaf militants were encamped. The villagers were said to be paid well for their silent support with the profits that the group accrued through hostage-taking and extortion.

Abu Sayyaf was largely restricted to the Sulu peninsula, as was its parent organization, the MNLF, which also had its strength in this area. Elsewhere in Mindanao there were also extremist wings of the Moro movement, especially in central and northern regions of Mindanao where the MILF was dominant. As mentioned earlier, the Bangsamoro Islamic Freedom Fighters, allied with ISIS. Based in central Mindanao, in the Maguindanao area, BIFF engaged in several attacks on outposts of the Philippine army and special forces in that region, challenging the authority of the MILF.

Another ISIS-affiliated splinter organization was the Maute group, which was based in the province of Lanao del Sur, the area surrounding Lake Lanao in northern Mindanao. The city of Marawi is the capital of the province. The group was founded in 2012 as a kind of family business by two brothers, Abdullah Jakul Maute and Omar Maute, and their sister, Jorge Salsalani. Much of their funding came from their mother, Ominta Romato Maute, who operated a construction company. The brothers had been members of the MILF and became disaffected with the movement's turn towards negotiations with the government. They gathered a sizable group of perhaps a couple of hundred disaffected MILF fighters and launched attacks on the government security forces in the Lanao del Sur region. In 2015 the Maute brothers declared their allegiance to ISIS, and in 2016 launched an attack far from their base in Lanao del Sur; they set off a bomb in a night market in Davao City that killed fifteen and wounded seventy.

Though allegedly an ISIS-related group, the Maute brothers group, like Abu Sayyaf, the Bangsamoro Islamic Freedom Fighters, and other groups in Mindanao that have latched onto the ISIS name, is an example of ISIS-branding. It had no real connection to the ISIS movement but had adopted its name to give it international militant credibility. Nonetheless, it and the other ISIS-branded movements in Mindanao were just as lethal within their own locale as ISIS was in Syria and Iraq. Any of these movements in Mindanao had the ability to erupt in violence if it sensed that the mood of frustration in the Muslim regions would support them.

This is exactly what the more moderate leaders of the Moro movement feared. As the months and years dragged on and the MILF-negotiated peace agreement remained unratified, the credibility of the main movement waned and the radical ISIS-related splinter groups began to gain strength. The worries that Butch Malang expressed to me regarding the potential for future violence turned out to be tragically prescient.

It would not be long before this potential became realized. By 2016 the two main ISIS-related groups, the Maute brothers' group and Abu Sayyaf, began to coordinate their efforts. They formed a plan to take hostage an entire city, and the result was the spectacular raid on the city of Marawi in 2017.

The Marawi Apocalypse

In May 2017, the former MILF militant Naguib Sinarimbo left his wife and twenty-year-old son in the town of Marawi in northern Mindanao while he traveled to Davao City on business, two hundred miles away. Naguib told me that he was confident that they would be safe since Marawi was where he had attended college at Mindanao State University, and where many friends and family were located.[11] His son was enrolled in college there at the same university that Naguib had attended, and was studying the coping mechanisms of displaced persons in the area's recent floods. Naguib's wife was helping him with some of the interviews for the project.

That's when all hell broke loose.[12] Naguib began receiving frantic text messages from his wife, son, and friends in Marawi. The Maute brothers gang had joined forces with Abu Sayyaf and established themselves in the center of the old city near the main mosque, defying the government to remove them. They had established perimeter security lines around the old city, essentially making hostages out of the entire town. The initial efforts of the Philippine police to break through the lines were unsuccessful. The warriors with the Maute brothers gang knew the city well, and had created tunnels and back-alley exits to avoid the government forces at some times and at other times to entrap them. The government had decided to call in the army.

For Naguib this was a personal matter. His wife and son were there. He immediately got into a car and started driving on what is ordinarily a five- or six-hour journey. The road was jammed, however, with people trying to leave Marawi; Naguib was one of the few going the other way. Eventually he made it into the city, and what he found was an urban area under siege. The roadblocks were chaotic, some erected by the government forces, some by the rebels. Naguib was able to make his way around the roadblocks and found his wife and son, who were in hiding. He managed to take them to a relatively safer part of the city.

For a month Naguib and his family were sequestered, with little access to food and outside contact while the fighting raged all around them. He had only the three shirts that he had brought with him to Davao City, and the family survived on canned sardines and dry noodles. When they had the opportunity to move, they shifted to a safer place in the outskirts of the old city near Mindanao State University. They stayed in the area in part so that Naguib could help with relief efforts, setting up a civilian response center and helping to locate civilians trapped in the city. He was able to negotiate with both the rebels and the army, since some of the former fighters from MILF whom Naguib knew had joined forces with the rebels, and since the head of the combined government forces was General Carlito Galvez. The general had previously been posted in Cotabato City, where he was associated with the negotiating team from MILF that included Naguib, and had been involved in setting up the Coordinating Committee for the Cessation of Hostilities. Thus Naguib could be an intermediary, a role that he attempted to use to free a Catholic priest whom the rebels were holding for ransom, and to try to persuade the government to be less heavy-handed in its assault on the rebel outposts since they were destroying large parts of the old city in the process.

Ultimately Naguib was not very successful in either of these negotiating attempts. The priest and other captives were able to flee by themselves when the army tear-gassed the mosque where they were being held captive. And General Galvez capitulated to pressure to try to end the siege by calling in air strikes that further damaged the city. Naguib said that he had told General Galvez that if they engaged in a protracted air battle the destruction would be catastrophic, and public sentiment would turn against the government. In fact that turned out to be the case when the battle went on for five months before the city was reclaimed—or what was left of if after the all-out airborne military assault.

It is not clear why Abu Sayyaf and the Maute brothers took over the city. Naguib speculated that one of the leaders of Abu Sayyaf, Abu Dhar, wanted to temporarily seize power just to demonstrate that they could do it, and then quickly leave. The idea was to perform a show of strength that would attract funds from the international ISIS network and recruits from Mindanao youth. According to Naguib, they intended to control the city only a day or two and then depart, but then they got trapped by the government muslim forces. Other reports indicate that security forces simply stumbled on a gathering of rebel forces and surprised them. The government's security forces did not want them to leave quickly, since they thought that this would be an opportune moment to get rid of two terrorist groups—Abu Sayyaf and the Maute brothers gang—cornered by government forces in the city. The assumption was that they were sitting ducks and could be easily done in. This turned out to be a grave error, since the rebels knew the city well and slipped into hiding places that made their capture almost impossible. It took five months and air power that destroyed the city before they were eradicated.

Other people with whom I spoke thought that the rebels had other motives. Some thought that they really did want to establish an Islamic State in northern Mindanao with Marawi as the capital. Both of the groups had pledged support to Abu Bakr al-Baghdadi as Caliph of the Islamic State, and starting with the takeover of Marawi they hoped to gain an outpost for ISIS in the Philippines. Still others with whom I spoke thought their intentions were purely mercenary. According to them, the rebels had posed a ransom price of some ten million dollars to free the city, but the government showed no interest in negotiating.

Whatever their intentions in seizing the city, once they were there the government forces quickly put up a perimeter border to keep them from leaving. Some rebels were able to depart since, especially at night, they could sneak out, often by taking a boat across the lake to areas not held by the government forces. Abu Dhar, one of the Abu Sayyaf leaders, left in the initial days of the conflict, and the Maute brothers' mother also escaped by boat across the lake. But the two Maute brothers, Omar and Abdullah, along with Isnilon Hapilon, the main leader of Abu Sayyaf, refused to leave the city. Naguib speculated that since Hapilon's wife and daughter were killed in a police encounter in the mosque in the old city of Marawi during the first days of the conflict, he had decided he had nothing to lose and would go down fighting. Moreover, the leaders might have thought that they would lose credibility with their movements if they left while their own militia continued to battle the government forces. According to Naguib they had also lost whatever support they had from the local residents, many of whom blamed them for bringing on the rain of fire that destroyed the town, so it became increasingly difficult for the rebel leaders to move about without being reported to the authorities.

One resident of Marawi told me that on the second day of the fighting the army chased the ISIS fighters out of a school that they had occupied, and then the army unit occupied it themselves in a kind of bivouac. Unknown to them, two ISIS fighters had not been driven out but were hiding under the floor. They emerged one night when the unit was sleeping and systematically killed them all. After that, the Marawi resident said, the army decided to bring in air power to attack ISIS strongholds instead of using human personnel in door-to-door combat.

The decision to use air power had a devastating effect on the city. Building after building became the target for military airstrikes, and as the siege turned into months, the Philippine military called for reinforcements. They requested the so-called "bunker-buster" bombs from the American military to strike deeply under the surface to kill militants who were hiding in basements and deep spaces underground. And they also requested drones with night-vision cameras to track the movements of the militant groups at night.

Eventually the government forces won. By October 23, 2017, the fighting ended. All of the leaders, including Abu Sayyaf's Hapilon and the two Maute brothers, had been killed, along with hundreds of their fighting militia members. Naguib's estimate, based on reports from inside the city, was that no more than three hundred rebel fighters were involved in the battle, two hundred of whom were killed and another hundred escaped. According to the government, however, almost a thousand rebels were killed and an unknown number may have fled; the government reports claimed that only 168 government soldiers were killed, though Naguib says that the actual number was much higher. He claims that the government wanted to make it look like the rebel forces were a greater opponent than they in fact were, and that the government forces took fewer losses than in fact they did. For that reason, according to Naguib, the government exaggerated the numbers of rebel fighters and slighted the number of government troops that were injured or killed. Both local observations and official government reports acknowledged that there were foreigners among the rebels—thirteen from Malaysia, Indonesia, Saudi Arabia, and elsewhere, though none from the heartland of ISIS in Iraq or Syria. Regardless of what the actual numbers were on both sides, there is no question that this was the longest and most deadly urban battle that the independent Philippines had ever faced. It was the heaviest fighting on Filipino soil since World War II.

After Marawi

The anger over Marawi's decimation was palpable when I visited it a few months later. Viewing the old city from across the lake gave a panorama of destruction that was truly disturbing. Not a single building appeared to have been untouched. The government did succeed in its goal of routing the ISIS-related militants, many of whom were killed in the battle. Some of the Maute-Abu Sayyaf fighters had survived the Marawi conflict, but where the survivors went was somewhat unclear.

I got some sense about where the remaining militants might be hiding when I hired a car to take me from Cotabato City to Marawi. It is less than a hundred miles on reasonably good paved highway, and ordinarily it would take about four hours for the journey. I had arranged for a driver who knew the area well, and who also had a sense of the dangers that might be around us. We had to drive through wooded mountain areas near Lake Lanao that, according to my driver, contained the hideouts of some of the remaining militants. The road was virtually empty, and the fact that few other vehicles dared to be driving there should have been a warning. Every ten miles or so there was an army checkpoint, which I found to be reassuring.

At the first checkpoint they asked to see my passport, and by the time we got to the second checkpoint they already knew that I was coming. "This is good," I said to my driver, who hesitantly agreed that it was good—if in fact the soldiers who checked me were calling ahead to other soldiers and not to the rebels. I suddenly realized what he meant: any of the checkpoints could have been set up by a militia eager to kidnap a foreigner for ransom money. "If we are stopped by the rebels," my driver said, "they will take you and hold you for ransom; but in my case they will just kill me on the spot."

With this incentive my driver drove as fast as he could. It was one of the scariest journeys I have ever taken. The speed and jarring of the road left me shaken and nauseated. Fortunately we arrived safely in Marawi well under the four hours allocated for the trip, and I was able to rest for a bit and catch my breath.

I didn't rest for long, however, since I had a list of MILF-related contacts in the city whom I wanted to meet. I wanted to get a sense of how they viewed the incident that had left the city in shambles, and what they thought the impact of the battle would now have on the extreme militant movement and on the peace process.

"There's nothing left," a former resident of Marawi told me, showing videos on his cell phone of the site of his family home in the center of the old city.[13] He had taken the videos himself several days earlier. He was right about there being nothing left—I could see only a pile of brick and stone rubble where he said that a multi-story building once had proudly stood.

"My mother built that home with her sweat and toil," he said sadly. She had worked for years as a domestic housekeeper in Saudi Arabia, carefully sending the earnings back to her family in the Philippines. Part of the money was for their college education. The rest was for the house in Marawi. Finally, after forty years of domestic labor abroad, she returned to Marawi several years before the siege. Her plan was to spend her retirement years with her extended family in the house that she had lovingly built with her remittance funds over all those years. It had a stone façade and metal grill-work, her son told me. And it was located directly across from the main mosque in the center of the city.

That turned out to be its undoing. On May 23, 2017, a group of the separatist rebels barricaded themselves inside the mosque. Seeing the army and militants coming into her neighborhood, his mother, along with most of the residents of the city, fled as reinforcements came from both sides. The roads were packed with terrified, fleeing residents. As they looked behind they could see parts of buildings crumbling in the pitched battle between the militants and the Philippines armed forces.

The physical damage to the city was devastating. Not only was the mother's house and the rest of the area immediately around the mosque destroyed, but virtually all of the inner city was left in ruins. The mother of the Marawi resident with whom I spoke was not an ISIS militant, of course. She was just a returning domestic worker. Her son, my conversation partner, had benefitted from her education funds. He finished college and earned a PhD, and was now a working professional in the city. Though not a rebel, he was a Muslim and sympathetic with the goal of semi-autonomy for the Mindanao region and had played a role in the past in helping to negotiate between the government and rebel groups.

A large percent of the former residents with whom I spoke blamed the army for the decimation of the city. They were bitter about the physical damage to their buildings, and also about the breakdown in civil order. Even buildings that were not destroyed were often looted. Some of the looting was undoubtedly done by the ISIS militants, but some residents told me that even in areas that were not controlled by ISIS, but where the army had required mandatory evacuation, there was looting. They blamed this on the army. "We lost a computer and two televisions," one Marawi resident told me.

Several of the local Marawi residents complained that they had not been told how the damage would be repaired and how compensation would be arranged. They insisted that this was the responsibility of the Philippine government.[14] Regardless of who one might blame for causing the conflict, it was clear that the property damage was inflicted primarily by army missile attacks. Several citizen committees were demanding immediate restitution. They were frustrated by the slow response to the enormity of the devastation.

One former Moro activist was even angrier. He had helped to launch protest movements and investigative reporting into what he claimed was widespread corruption among the fledgling restitution efforts that the government had provided. Very few people who lived in the destroyed areas of the old city had access to the documents that would prove their property rights; in many cases they had passed on their property from generation to generation without any documentation. For this reason the government had provided funds to anyone who claimed to have lived in the city. This approach, the activist told me, was subject to abuse as the government officials were giving the money to friends of theirs who would give them a kickback. He wanted to know why the government didn't use earlier versions of Google maps to identify properties that could be verified by the witness of neighbors, if not by government documents, to diminish the possibility of corruption.

Hence many residents resented the government—both for being the agent of destruction of their property and for what they felt was an inadequate response to their loss and their demands for restitution. But a deeper problem also lay in the wake of the army's destruction of the city: the rise of a new militancy.

Already many young Muslims in the region were turning to a more militant expression of Muslim political power due to the frustration caused by the stalemate in the peace process. Now the destruction of Marawi by the military gave a new impetus to these anti-government sentiments and stoked the fires of radicalism. Not all of the members of the movement had been killed in the encounter, and stories were circulating about how they had retreated to the mountains near the road where I had traveled the day before. There, the local residents told me, the numbers of militants were expanding. They were joined, I was told, by many young men from Marawi and the surrounding region.

"Older people like me can see both sides," I was told by a resident who had supported the Moro movements for many years. He explained that he and others his age could see that the army was trapped and it was a lose-lose situation for both sides in the Marawi standoff. "But younger people," he said, with concern in his voice, "they don't see the broader picture." He also said that the army's recourse to air power rather than fighting man-to-man in a house-to-house combat gave the army the appearance of being weak and unmanly in the eyes of many of the young men in the city, who felt that they should have fought directly rather than from behind the shield of technology.

The old activist told me about a conversation he had had with the son of one of his neighbors, a thirteen-year-old boy whose house had been destroyed in the fighting. He was angry at the army, the boy said, adding that when he was older he planned to join ISIS. He wanted to get an M-14 rifle, he said, and hunt down the Philippine tank driver who had destroyed his home and kill him. In telling this story, the activist cautioned that this was an initial response from an immature boy and as the boy became older he might see the world through calmer eyes. He also thought that it was unlikely that the Maute brothers' gang and Hapilon's Abu

Sayyaf could survive intact without their charismatic leaders. Still, he thought it quite possible that a new extremist movement would emerge among the young people who were enraged over the destruction of Marawi. "It might be a new radical movement," he said darkly, "one that is less concerned about religion and is instead fueled by a deeply anti-government sentiment."

When I returned to Manila the next week I had dinner with a former student of mine, a native Filipino from the southern part of the islands who was then working with the United Nation's Children's Fund, UNICEF, which had erected a number of relief camps in the area around Marawi to help the refugees. My former student had been there and met with many young people in their early teens, and in talking with them he tried to avoid any topics that were political or that would evoke traumatic memories. He would ask them about the future, what they would like to do when they grew up, he said.[15]

"We want to join the militants," a majority told him as my former student tried to hide his shocked look of surprise. He did not know whether the teenagers' anger would last, or whether it would propel them into active participation in a radical movement. But he was worried. It would appear that although the Philippine army had destroyed the city, the war was far from over.

Negotiating for Peace

This prognosis for continuing conflict was also the view of Major Carlos Sol, the director of the government-sponsored Coordinating Committee for the Cessation of Hostilities. He represented the government side of the coordination leadership alongside Butch Malang, the MILF guerilla commander with whom I had also met, who served as the vice-director of the Coordinating Committee. Major Sol, though a former Philippines army officer, was raised in Mindanao, knew the leaders of the Moro movement and their concerns well, and could literally speak their language. He and his rebel counterpart, Butch Malang, seemed to be not only colleagues in the peace process, but friends.

When I first talked with Major Sol in 2016 he was guardedly optimistic about the progress towards peace in the region.[16] The years of government negotiation with the MILF had resulted in a peace agreement to replace the existing Autonomous Region in Muslim Mindanao with a new entity, Bangsamoro. It would give greater self-rule to the Muslim community in the region and provide for a distribution of government funds to support it. On March 27, 2014, the Comprehensive Agreement on the Bangsamoro was signed in Manila in the presence of Philippines President Benigno Aquino and MILF Chairman Al Haj Murad Ibrahim. It looked like peace was around the corner.

But it wasn't, and that's why Major Sol's optimism was guarded. Before the agreement could come into effect it had to be ratified through a referendum of the populace in the region and by the Philippines legislature. Since the MILF leadership supported it, the referendum seemed likely to be approved by the local Mindanao population. As mentioned earlier, the Philippines legislature, however, was another story. It sat on the proposal without acting on it. As the months turned to years the people in the region became restless.

When I talked with Major Sol in 2016, he said that if the agreement was not ratified within a year, extremist elements would emerge and create a new wave of violence. When I talked with Butch Malang about the situation he was more specific.[17] The Bangsamoro Islamic Freedom Fighters (BIFF) had already split off from the MILF over the main movement's willingness to negotiate with the government. The longer the agreement stayed in limbo, unimplemented, the greater the chance that BIFF would gain strength. The MILF leadership was losing credibility, Butch Malang told me, and younger supporters especially were getting impatient, and willing to take more radical steps if the inaction continued. Moreover, both Major Sol and Butch Malang told me, there was an even darker cloud over the horizon. Some leaders of BIFF were negotiating with ISIS, and the radical movement in the Sulu peninsula, Abu Sayyaf, was already openly acknowledging its ISIS connections. With the ISIS ideology came the justification for savage acts of violence and the possibility of international support, both with personnel and money. Thus the inaction was not just frustrating, it was potentially explosive.

Sure enough, less than a year later, in 2017, when the Philippines legislature did nothing to ratify the agreement, fighting began again. As predicted, it was led by extremist forces, some of which were connected with ISIS. The result was Marawi. As the ISIS-related Moro movements, Abu Sayyaf and the Maute brothers gang, took over the city and waged its five-month battle with the Philippine army, the two main Moro movements, the Moro National Liberation Front and the Moro Islamic Liberation Front, both tried to stay out of the battle. They tried to keep their own supporters in line, even though extreme elements from both organizations had joined forces with Abu Sayyaf and the Maute brothers in their conquest of the city. To show they were not supporting the ISIS rebels, both the MNLF and MILF offered to provide military support for the Philippine army, though their offer was not accepted. As I have mentioned, the MILF leader Naguib Sinarimbo, who was in Marawi at the time of the battle, played a role as a go-between, attempting to negotiate between the rebels and the government troops. When I talked with Butch Malang in 2018, he told me that the MILF helped to create a "peace corridor" supported by both militants and the army that allowed hundreds of innocent civilians caught in the fighting to escape the city.

When the fighting ended, the resentment over the destruction of Marawi remained. Moreover, the peace agreement still was unsigned, and the sorrow over the decimation of the city was compounded with the frustration over progress on the peace agreement that would have given hope for the future. Some young people joined the rebels in the mountain to continue the fight.

"What peace process is there?," a teenage son of a friend of Naguib Sinarimbo asked him cynically in the months after the Marawi battle.[18] The young man had been quiet through the months of the battle, but now that it was over he felt emboldened to challenge his elders on the failed promise of their years of negotiating efforts. Like many in his generation, the teenager blamed the army for the destruction, rather than ISIS.

Days after the conversation, the lawyer told me, the boy disappeared. His family feared that he had joined the ISIS-affiliated rebels. Naguib told me that he blamed himself for not doing more to try to persuade the young man that the peace process between the Muslim separatists and the Philippine government was still worthwhile. In July 2018 President Rodrigo Duterte finally signed the agreement that had been negotiated four years before, but it was too late to save the teenager from joining the armed rebels.

During my last conversation with Butch Malang, the old MILF commander who became the co-chair of the Coordinating Committee for the Cessation of Hostilities, he was accompanied by a young college-aged man working as a volunteer with the MILF

Youth Outreach Program. His job was to reach out to young people like the teenager who had spurned the peace process after the Marawi battle and joined the militants in the hills.

I asked the outreach volunteer what he did to try to turn the minds of young people away from war. He said that part of his effort was related to religion, telling them that true Islam is for peace and nonviolence and not for fighting. Islam, he said, was all about civil order. But he also wanted them to be realistic, to realize that the efforts to confront the government violently had only led to failure and death. For that, he said, all he had to do was point to what happened at Marawi.[19]

What happened at Marawi, I said, was a destructive conflict that had turned many of the young people, including the teenage son of Naguib's friend, against the government and spurred them into militancy. The young volunteer agreed, and said that he concurred with their anger. But he wanted them to channel it in a direction that would lead to peace and not to more conflict.

I said that he had a difficult job, and the volunteer nodded yes, and admitted that not everyone with whom he talked was persuaded. He personally knew several who had turned their backs on him and joined the militants despite his efforts. Still, he said, he had to keep trying. There was no alternative to peace, he said.

After the Marawi conflict was over, it became apparent throughout the Philippines that the militants frustrated by the inability of the Philippine legislature to ratify the 2014 peace agreement and create a Bangsamoro autonomous region in Mindanao. Finally President Rodrigo Duterte pressured the legislature to act, and on July 26, 2018, Duterte was able to sign the landmark agreement. The only thing left to complete the approval of the agreement was a referendum vote of the residents in the areas of Mindanao that were to be part of the agreement. That took place in the following year, and easily passed. On May 10, 2019, in Cotabato City, an official signing took place that marked the end of four decades of fighting that had left 120,000 people dead. The agreement called for the new Bangsamoro autonomous region to have its own parliament, with a portion of the taxes from the region allocated to support it. The thirty to forty thousand MILF fighters would relinquish their weapons, and new political parties contesting in parliamentary elections would replace the paramilitary forces of the organization. I was impressed to see that the old Moro militant, Naguib Sinarimbo, was made Minister of the Interior, the de facto administrator of the new Bangsamoro government.

The pictures of the 2019 signing that were published in newspapers throughout the country showed a smiling Butch Malang, the former commander representing the guerilla forces of the MILF, seated next to the chairman of the Philippines Armed Forces, Brigadier General Cirilo Thomas Donato, Jr. This remarkable portrayal of two old enemies seated together at the agreement table was testimony to something that Malang had told me in one of my conversations with him months before. "From now on," he said, "all problems can be solved by peace."[20]

4   *The Fight for Khalistan in India's Punjab*

When my colleague at Guru Nanak Dev University in Amritsar, Professor Jagrup Singh Sekhon, asked if I wanted to go and visit Wassan Singh Zaffarwal, at first I didn't believe what I was hearing. "*The* Zaffarwal?" I asked, tentatively.

Yes, Prof. Sekhon said, explaining that Zaffarwal was living on his family farm near the town of Batala in Gurdaspur district. It was only an hour's drive north of Amritsar, he said. Did I want to go?

"Of course," I answered. It was if someone had offered me the chance to visit with General Vo Nguyan Giap, the head of the North Vietnamese forces, after the end of the Vietnam War. Zaffarwal was just that significant.

Years ago when I started my studies of the rise of religious-related violent movements around the world, I began with the area that I knew best, the Punjab, and the Khalistan movement that had seized the countryside throughout the 1980s. At that time one of the largest and most violent groups was the Zaffarwal branch of the Khalistan Commando Force. It was an uncompromising and ferocious militia, and Zaffarwal himself was known as a hard and dedicated leader. It would have been impossible to meet with Zaffarwal then, even if you could find him, which would be unlikely since he was so closely guarded. I was surprised, quite frankly, that he was still alive, much less living unrestrained within the area in which he had once been a formidable rebel leader.

But there he was in his farmhouse north of Amritsar. Zaffarwal was a tall man in his late fifties, sporting a long white beard and a saffron-colored turban tied across the front, in the manner that the Khalistan leader Sant Jarnail Singh Bhindranwale preferred, rather than coming to a peak in the center, the way most Sikhs tie their turbans. The family compound in which he lived had a wall around the outside of a courtyard, which itself was surrounded by fields. When I was there the small compound was full of life. There were relatives of various ages and chickens running loose. Women were busy preparing the evening meal. Zaffarwal looked like the scion of a large rural family, which he was. The old radical Zaffarwal was something of a memory, but his recollections were still sharp as he told me his story.

The Rise and Fall of Wassan Singh Zaffarwal

Zaffarwal was born in 1959 in the area in which he now lives, and where his family developed the farm that he has inherited. He was a high school dropout, working in his late teens as a security guard for a large wool mill. But he had political ambitions. He hoped to win a leadership role in the union supported by the six thousand workers in the mill and use that platform to vault himself into a political career. He hoped someday to run for the state legislature.

The political unrest of the 1970s, however, led him a different direction. The Akali party was organizing protests against the government's policy regarding water rights, which the rural Sikhs thought was depriving them of their rightful resources. Zaffarwal kept up his involvement in the Akali protests into the 1980. So he was known to the police, he told me, as an agitator.

According to Zaffarwal's account, he initially had no interest in the Khalistan movement and never went to hear Bhindranwale, the Sikh leader.[1] Though some biographies of Zaffarwal state that he joined Bhindranwale's ashram, the Damdami Taksal, and was a follower of the Sant, Zaffarawal's testimony to me was quite different.[2] He said that his involvement with the movement occurred only after Bhindranwale was killed in the 1984 Indian army assault on Bhindranwale's encampment within the confines of the Golden Temple in Amritsar. The reason he joined, Zaffarwal said, was because of police harassment. After the Golden Temple attack, known as Operation Blue Star, the police were rounding up any suspected supporter of Bhindranwale and his guerrilla movement. Because Zaffarwal had been identified with political activism in the protests against the government's water policies, the police came after him. He was roughed up and brutally interrogated, Zaffarwal said, on two occasions. When he heard that they were coming to harass him again, Zaffarwal said that he went into hiding.

He was twenty-five years old at the time, and a fugitive. Zaffarwal said that he joined a network of other young runaways who were also fleeing police harassment. Some were supporters of Bhindranwale, some were suspected for what Zaffarwal described as no reason at all, except that they were young rural Sikh men, the sort who might have been Bhindranwale supporters. After they absconded, he said, they traipsed from village to village at night, and were protected by the villagers during the daytime. It was during this time, through his association with young Bhindranwale cadres, that Zaffarwal said he became educated in the idea of having a separate state of their own that would protect Sikhs.

He said that as he continued to stay in hiding, he become more involved in one of the main organizations in the movement, the Khalistan Liberation Army. As Zaffarwal became more active in the movement, his peers recognized his leadership qualities, and in January, 1986, when a coordinating committee was created to provide leadership for the post-Bhindrawale stage of the movement, Zaffarwal was appointed as one of the five founding members of the Panthic Committee ("the committee of the fellowship"). For Zaffarwal, this was the moment of political leadership for which he had been longing, and the vision of struggle they formulated was one to which he was totally dedicated. It was this group that met in the precincts of the Golden Temple in April 1986 to proclaim "A Declaration of the Independence of Khalistan," a separate Sikh state, before an assembly of journalists. The five leaders of the Panthic Committee, including Zaffarwal, were all wanted men, so as soon as they made their announcement, while tea was being served to the journalists, they slipped outside and vanished before the police could arrive.[3]

The Panthic Committee largely consisted of those, like Zaffarwal, who were identified with the Damdami Taksal, though it also gained the support of the Sikh Students Federation, which was an important element of the rebel forces. It did not, however, include another group, the Babbar Khalsa, which was more conservative and religiously-specific in its requirements, including prohibiting women from wearing jeans or anything other than the traditional Punjabi women's outfit, *salwar-kameez,* which consisted of baggy trousers and a long shirt-like blouse. Initially the Panthic Committee also included a representative of the Bhindranwale Tiger Force of Khalistan, led by Gurbachan Singh Manochahal, though this group split from the committee in 1988.

By that time Zaffarwal was leading the major faction of the Panthic Committee and he was also assuming leadership of his own organization, the Khalistan Commando Force. The movement emerged out of the Khalistan Liberation Army. Manbir Singh Chaheru was proclaimed the founding leader in August 1985, but within days he was captured by the police and not heard from again. He was replaced by Sukhdev Singh (known as General Labh Singh), who was also killed by the police, and was succeeded in turn by Kanwarjit Singh Sultanwind. On October 18, 1989, the twenty-three-year old Sultanwind was cornered by the police and took a cyanide capsule to commit suicide. After that the Khalistan Commando Force broke into several factions, but the major one was led by Zaffarwal, and the organization was known as KCF-Zaffarwal. (Some reports say that Zaffarwal headed the major branch of the movement a year earlier, in 1988, after Labh Singh's death; others date its beginning as 1989, after Sultanwind died.) By 1989, the Khalistan Commando Force had broken into several rival groups, but the most prestigious was Zaffarwal's.

The KCF became notorious for the severity of its attacks, including assassinations of political and military figures. It also targeted prominent Hindu leaders who had denounced the rebels' violence. It was said to have financed its operations through extortion, looting, and bank robbery. One of the best-known attacks attributed to the KCF was the killing of General Arun Vaidya, who was the chief of the Indian Army and the architect of Operation Blue Star. The assassination was carried out by two young men, Sukhdev and Harjinder Singh, popularly known as "Sukha" and "Jinda."

Vaidya had taken up residence in the city of Pune, far from the Punjab, but the young men traveled to the state of Maharashtra specifically to carry out the assassination. Knowing Sikhs would stand out in the area, they shaved their beards and tried to look like ordinary twenty-four-year-old Hindu young men. On August 10, 1986, two years after Operation Blue Star, they were able to get into the retirement compound where the General lived, and as he was returning from the market the two friends rode up on a motorcycle beside his car and fired eight or nine shots into it, killing Vaidya instantly and severely wounding his wife.[4] Months later Sukha and Jinda were apprehended, tried, and convicted of murder. In 1992 they were executed in Pune. Since then they have been revered as martyrs throughout the Sikh community, where their smiling faces grace calendar art. They are regarded as having carried out an appropriate revenge for the Indian government's assault on the most sacred of Sikh shrines, the Golden Temple, which Sikhs know as the Darbar Sahib.

When I asked Zaffarwal about the killing, he said, correctly, that he was not the leader of the KCF at the time, though he understood why Sikhs would want to take revenge on General Vaidya. When I mentioned other attacks that were related to KCF at a later date, during the time of his leadership, Zaffarwal said that the organization was decentralized, and often rogue elements would carry out actions that were not under his control. Though this was likely true, it is also likely that Zaffarwal's comments to me were meant to distance himself from any of the KCF acts that could still get him into legal trouble.

The movement never attacked innocent people, Zaffarwal told me, only government officials and military leaders. He did admit that sometimes "boys" took matters into their own hands, including committing acts of revenge against individuals for personal reasons. But he had no control over this, he again asserted. Though he did not offer any examples of how the organization tried to discipline members in cases like this, Zaffarwal said that he "took notice" of what they had done. It was hard to control them, he said, adding that his troops were not a disciplined army but just a guerrilla band. When I asked where they got their weapons, he said that they were taken from police stations, and later through procuring smuggled weapons from Pakistan. But Zaffarwal insisted that the weapons were for defensive purposes only, or to attack the "enemy," by which he meant political and military leaders.

By the end of the 1980s, there was disunity throughout the rebel forces. The Panthic Committee was not able to gain control over the Babbar Khalsa, and even within Zaffarwal's own organization, the KCF, there were disagreements. It split into three groups, with Zaffarwal commanding the largest. After the Panthic Committee proclaimed Khalistan, Zaffarwal said, repression became even more severe. Fearing that the police were closing in on him, Zaffarwal decided to flee to Pakistan.

In 1987, according to Zaffarwal's account, he just walked over the border to the neighboring country. Pakistani officials there were pleased to welcome him and other Khalistan activists, Zaffarwal said. They provided them with food and housing, and enabled him to have the communications channels needed to continue his leadership of the movement. He continued to issue proclamations on behalf of the Panthic Committee, and to send directives to his branch of the KCF.

By 1995, however, the movement had largely dissolved or been destroyed by heavy-handed police tactics. Zaffarwal no longer had a movement to command. It was also possible that the Pakistani government was no longer supplying the kind of support that it had earlier. But without explaining exactly why, Zaffarwal said that he decided that the time had come to leave Pakistan. He was adjusting to the reality that the great struggle to which he had dedicated years of commitment was now over and would not soon return. He could not return to India without facing multiple legal charges, he said, so he decided to go to Switzerland. He was able to procure a fake passport, and flew to Zurich where he asked for and received political asylum. There he formed a network with other Khalistan expatriates who had fled to Switzerland.

In 2000 Zaffarwal decided to return to India. He went to Madrid, Spain, and applied to the Indian Consulate for a passport, claiming that his Indian passport had been lost (in fact he never had one). He was able to get a temporary passport that allowed him to return to India. At first he went into hiding in the Punjab. But eventually he was discovered by the police. Other accounts say that Zaffarwal returned from Switzerland to the Punjab on April 11, 2001, after negotiating his surrender.[5] Zaffarwal told me that on his return he was interrogated for two weeks and faced eleven counts of murder, treason, and other crimes. He was in jail for months awaiting the trial but when the time came, he said, all the charges were dropped for lack of evidence. Other accounts report that he was in fact convicted on two of the nine charges levied against him, and served two years in prison before being freed on bail.[6] Either way, however, Zaffarwal was soon a free man and able to return to the family farm where I met him. Still, he said, he continued to be pestered by police surveillance.

I asked him whether he was still in touch with his old comrades from the KCF days. He said he was not—though he probably would not have admitted to these contacts if he had had them. But he added that he was chagrined to find that on his return to India in 2000, most of his old comrades ignored him. They had moved on with their lives and did not want to be associated with the old militant leader.

Looking back on his experiences with the uprising of the 1980s, Zaffarwal said that he had few regrets. He was, however, deeply disappointed that the movement did not achieve any of its goals. Would the Khalistan movement return, I asked him? No, he said, because the Indian government had learned its lesson that heavy-handed police responses would only create a more severe reprisal. This left open the question of whether he thought that a separate Sikh state was needed, or whether it was justified. It was also unclear whether he would join it if in fact a new movement arose.

The Battle for Khalistan

Zaffarwal's story appears to be similar to those of many other leaders of the Sikh uprising in the 1980s. But there were in fact many other leaders, and many other factions. Like the Moro movement in Mindanao, the Khalistan movement in the Punjab was fragmented. Jagtar Singh, an Amritsar-based journalist who formerly wrote for the *Indian Express* and who had become a confidant of Sant Jarnail Singh Bhindranwale, called it a "non-movement." When I discussed this idea with the journalist, he said that rather than being a movement it was "a combination of different kinds of groups, each with its own agenda."[7] Some were for the idea of an independent Sikh state, a "Khalistan," and others were not. Bhindranwale never came out publicly for it, whereas Simranjit Singh Mann, a former police official who was accused of masterminding the assassination of Indira Gandhi, did advocate it. When I talked with Mann, he said he was continuing to rally support for an independent Khalistan. He was pleased, he said, that the Indian

Supreme Court had ruled that it was legal to openly advocate for a separate Sikh political entity.[8]

Though disparate, all the movements that were loosely identified under the Khalistan label during the Sikh uprising of the 1980s had several features in common. They were all extralegal entities that justified violence in an uprising against the state, a revolution that was portrayed by Bhindranwale and other leaders as a great struggle, animated by images of battle from Sikh history. These were in most cases images of cosmic war, a metaphysical conflict between good and evil, and an existential battle for the survival of Sikh culture. This image of warfare was not solely ideological or religious; it also had political and economic dimensions. There was a general feeling that the perceived loss of economic power of the rural Jat Sikhs in the Punjab was due to government neglect or, worse, an evil intent to destroy Jat Sikh power and legitimacy.

Hence the mood among Sikhs in rural Punjab was one of anger and humiliation that led to images of warfare in which the government was perceived to be the enemy. Although there was no consensus within the movement over the political goal—whether or not to demand a separate Khalistan state—they were united on one thing. According to Gurtej Singh, an intellectual in the movement and a close confidant of Bhindranwale, what they really wanted was "respect."[9] He told me that the Sikhs felt that the policies of the government had marginalized them and were trying to drown their sense of religious community within a sea of secularism.

The movement began over religious differences. In 1978 a clash erupted between a group of Sikhs and the Sant Nirankaris, a branch of a movement that had splintered from the Sikh tradition. The Sant Nirankaris followed its own lineage of gurus. The leader of the Sikhs attacking the Nirankaris at this time was Jarnail Singh, a young rural preacher who at an early age had joined the Damdami Taksal, a religious school associated with the great Sikh martyr Baba Deep Singh. Jarnail Singh eventually became its head and assumed the name of the previous leader, who had come from a village named Bhindran and was therefore called "Bhindranwale," meaning simply a person from Bhindran. Jarnail Singh Bhindranwale began to monitor religious standards in the surrounding Sikh society and found the Sant Nirankaris's worship of a living guru to be presumptuous and offensive. In the escalating violence between the two groups, lives were lost on both sides. In 1980 the Nirankari guru was assassinated. Some suspected Bhindranwale of being implicated in the crime, but he was not charged or convicted.

Soon Bhindranwale became busy with a new organization, the Dal Khalsa ("the group of the pure"), which was supported by the prime minister's younger son, Sanjay Gandhi, and other Congress Party leaders, including the president of India, Zail Singh. They hoped that the group would split Sikh loyalties and undercut support for the largely Sikh political party the Akali Dal, a competitor for the Congress Party in the Punjab and the leading political voice of Punjabi Sikhs. But if these Congress Party leaders helped to create Bhindranwale's power, they would later regret it and consider that they had created a Frankenstein. The next year, the publisher of a chain of Hindu newspapers in Punjab who had been a critic of Bhindranwale was shot dead. Again, Bhindranwale was implicated, but never tried or convicted. In response to his arrest and the destruction of his personal papers, Bhindranwale turned against the government. Bands of young Sikhs began indiscriminately targeting Hindus, police and government officials; later in 1981 a group of Sikhs hijacked an Indian Airlines plane in Pakistan. The serious violence had begun.

The situation came to a head on June 5, 1984, when Indira Gandhi sent troops into the Golden Temple (the Darbar Sahib) in what was code-named Operation Blue Star, led by General Arun Vaidya. In a messy military operation that took two days to complete, two thousand or more people were killed, including a large number of innocent worshippers. Bhindranwale's forces put up a spirited defense, but eventually they were all killed, including the leader himself. What shocked the Sikh community was not only his death but also the desecration of their most sacred shrine by the Indian army.[10] Even moderate Sikhs throughout the world were horrified at the specter of soldiers' boots stomping through their holiest precincts, and the bullet holes in the buildings' elaborate marblework facades. The assassination of Mrs. Gandhi on October 31, 1984, was widely regarded as revenge for this act of profanity. On the following day more than two thousand Sikhs were massacred in Delhi and elsewhere by angry mobs—a reprisal orchestrated, some say, by the police themselves.[11] Two years later, as I mentioned earlier, General Vaidya was killed by the young Sikh militants Sukha and Jinda.

The sermons of Bhindranwale offer clues to his religious sensibilities and their political implications. In a rambling, folksy manner, he called on his followers to maintain their faith in a time of trial, and he echoed the common fear that Sikhs would lose their identity in a flood of resurgent Hinduism, or worse, in a sea of secularism. One of his more familiar themes was the survival of the Sikh community; for "community" he used the term *qaum*, which carries overtones of nationhood. As for the idea of Khalistan, a separate Sikh nation, Bhindranwale said he "neither favored it nor opposed it."[12] What Bhindranwale did support was the Sikh concept of *miri-piri*, the notion that spiritual and temporal power are linked. He projected the image of a great war between good and evil waged in the present day—"a struggle . . . for our faith, for the Sikh nation, for the oppressed."[13] He implored his young followers to rise up and marshal the forces of righteousness. "The Guru will give you strength," he assured them.[14]

Violence was not the explicit theme of Bhindranwale's messages, but he did not shrink from what he felt the implications of *miri-piri* might be in an unjust world. He affirmed that the Sikh tradition, like most religious traditions, ordinarily applauds nonviolence and proscribes the taking of human life. He acknowledged that "for a Sikh it is a great sin to keep weapons and kill anyone." But Bhindranwale went on to justify the occasional violent act in extraordinary circumstances and said that "it is an even greater sin to have weapons and not to seek justice."[15] In an extreme moment, he praised his young lieutenants for hijacking an airplane and called for either full concessions to his demands from India's political leaders, "or their heads."[16]

During its heyday in the 1980s, thousands of young men and perhaps a few hundred women joined the movement. They were initiated into the secret fraternities of various rival radical organizations. These included the Babbar Khalsa, the Khalistan Commando Force, the Khalistan Liberation Force, the Bhindranwale Tiger Force of Khalistan, and extremist factions of the All-India Sikh Students Federation. Their enemies were secular political leaders, heads of police units, some Hindu journalists, and other community leaders. Over time the distinctions between valid and inappropriate targets became blurred, and virtually anyone could become a victim of the militants' wrath. By January 1988, more than a hundred people a month were killed; 1991 was the bloodiest year, with over six thousand people killed in the Punjab's triangular battle among the police, the radicals, and the populace.[17] Official estimates state that a total of twenty thousand were killed during the uprising, and the actual numbers may be higher.[18] One of the more spectacular incidents was the attack by Sikh extremists on the Indian ambassador to Romania in Bucharest in 1991. The Romanian government helped to capture the Sikh assassins. They were killed, and later that year militant Sikhs kidnapped a Romanian diplomat in Delhi in retaliation.

Accompanying the increase in violence was a general collapse of law and order, especially in rural areas of the state near the Pakistani border. The young activists had intimidated the older Sikh leaders, who became virtual pawns of the militants. The only authority in some areas came from those who ruled by gun at night. This was due in part to the erosion of idealism in the Sikh movement and in part to the movement's exploitation by what amounted to street gangs and roving bands of thugs. In time, the Sikh movement had failed to achieve whatever political goals it might have espoused, including the dream of an independent Khalistan, leaving a cynical and demoralized public in its wake. In the absence of a legitimate government in the Punjab, the rural area became a no-man's-land in the battle between militants and armed police.

In the 1990s older and more responsible leaders in the Jat Sikh community found themselves in a quandary. They could not capitulate to the urban Hindu leadership of the central government because that would mean abandoning their religion and caste. They needed the young Sikh militants' support, but at the same time they wanted to regain some semblance of political control over them. One might think that it would be in the best interests of the central government to help them do that, but the Congress Party leaders were hesitant. For one thing, they resented the fact that moderate Sikh leaders identified with the Sikh Akali Party rather than the Congress Party or one of the national coalition parties. More important, they feared that any concessions they made to Sikh leaders would have repercussions throughout India. Muslims would immediately demand similar rights, as would leaders of separatist movements in northeastern India and Kashmir. Although the Sikh and Kashmiri separatist movements were not related, any concessions made to the former would certainly have been demanded by the latter, and vice versa. At the same time, the Indian government could not be too harsh on one group without affecting their dealings with the other. In the same week in 1995 that Punjab's chief minister, Beant Singh, was assassinated, for example, the Indian government was involved in delicate negotiations for the release of foreign hostages in Kashmir and could not have afforded renewed hostilities with the Sikhs.

The rise of Hindu nationalism in India coincided with the decline of the Sikh movement. In the 1990s the Hindu nationalist Bhartiya Janata Party ("Indian People's Party," commonly known as the BJP) began to gain strength in several northern Indian states, culminating in the formation of a national coalition government in 1998. At that time, some moderate factions of the Akali Party joined forces in alliance with the BJP. But these Akali-BJP coalitions achieved greater electoral success among the urban constituencies, which were both Hindu and Sikh, than in the rural Sikh strongholds. The suspicion of rural Sikhs toward Hindu politics, like the hatred between many activist Sikhs and the secular Congress Party, was never completely overcome.

In 1990, in a poignant attempt to break the vicious cycle of hatred and reprisal, the Congress prime minister, Rajiv Gandhi, in what was virtually his last act of office, released Simranjit Singh

Mann from prison. This was an extraordinary act, since Mann was awaiting trial for his alleged participation in the plot that had led to the murder of Rajiv's mother, Indira Gandhi. Mann had won a parliamentary seat after campaigning from prison, but Rajiv claimed that his pardon was due not to Mann's electoral success but to his own desire to "heal wounds."[19]

According to Simranjit Singh Mann, the tide began to turn against the militants in 1992. They were, in his opinion, destroyed from within as much as from without. It was a problem of leadership, Mann told me. When many of the leaders were captured, they were enjoying the fruits of their spoils, using air conditioners and driving expensive cars. "They advocated puritanical ways to the masses," Mann told me, "but they lived in luxury themselves."[20] The standards within the movement degenerated. "Guns controlled the party," he said, adding that "it should have been the other way around." Internal disputes were endemic, and many of the militants were killed by members of rival factions rather than by the police. In the late 1990s Mann was among the few activists who had not been killed, jailed, or sent into hiding abroad—mostly in Pakistan, England, and the United States. Like the former militants with whom I talked in India and the United States, Mann expressed bitterness at both the Indian government, which he felt had persecuted the movement, and the extremist members of the militant cadres, who he believed had destroyed the movement from within.

I asked Mann if he thought the militancy of the movement was a mistake. He said that given the geography of the Punjab, surrounded by the rest of India with its vastly superior military resources, the movement could not have launched a productive military venture—with the exception of those instances where "punishment" and "retribution" called for violence, as in the assassinations of prime minister Indira Gandhi and chief minister Beant Singh. But in most other cases, he said, the violence was counterproductive, in that it provided the government with a reason for exterminating the movement. Mann would have much preferred a peaceful solution, such as the one proposed for the separation of Quebec from Canada. But, Mann said, he was not opposed in principle to the use of force for a righteous cause. His disagreement with the use of violence in this instance was not "a moral decision," he said, "but a strategic one."[21]

One of the surviving leaders of the movement concurred that violence was sanctioned in Sikhism, but ordinarily as a defensive act. Sohan Singh, whose name is associated with one of the main coordinating bodies of the militant Sikh movement—the Sohan Singh Panthic Committee—was in his eighties when I visited him in the suburb of Mohali near Chandigarh.[22] He had devised a board on a wheel in his backyard which he showed me proudly, saying that it allowed one to be strapped on and elevated so one's blood ran towards one's head. He attributed his longevity to this device. He also spoke eloquently about the role of love in Sikhism, saying that the tradition emphasizes love and allows for conversion only through moral suasion.

Though Sohan Singh appeared to be just another charming old man, his past leadership role in the Panthic Committee belied this impression. In my conversation with him, Sohan Singh admitted that if others try to kill you, you are warranted in trying to kill them. He argued that the violence of the Sikhs in the 1980s was primarily a response to the violence of the state. Sohan Singh claimed that the killings undertaken by militants were always done for a purpose; they were "not killing for killing's sake."[23] Moreover, Sohan Singh said that warnings were given and punishment was meted out only if the offenders persisted in the conduct that the militants regarded as offensive.

One might wonder why the militants felt they had the moral authority to make judgments about others and to carry out corporal punishment on their own. In a remarkable series of interviews with Sikh militants transcribed and analyzed by Cynthia Keppley Mahmood in her book *Fighting for Faith and Nation,* the militants seemed unconcerned about the issue of their moral authority.[24] According to Sikh tradition, a council of five leaders is sufficient to give the community guidance; there is no hierarchy of priests or codified authority within Sikhism. In 1986, shortly after Bhindranwale was killed, the militants created their own Panthic Committee (an authoritative committee led by five elders). One of the members of this first committee, Bhai Dhanna Singh, told Mahmood that the task of the group was to speak for Sikhs. He said the term *Sikh* meant anyone "who listens to the Guru's command." This, Dhanna Singh said, was "to speak against injustice." He added that "anyone who complies with an oppressive regime is never a Sikh."[25]

Thus the militants claimed a divinely-ordained authority to right injustice and secure public order. Sohan Singh assumed that he and his colleagues had the moral jurisdiction to make life-and-death decisions about their constituency, especially when they thought that the government was morally bankrupt. What needed to be shown, he said, was that he and his colleagues were able to conduct their public role as upholders of political righteousness in a responsible manner. As an indication of what Sohan Singh considered to be the militants' good manners, he cited the apology they had extended to the families of those who were inadvertently killed in the explosion that took the life of Punjab's chief minister, Beant Singh, whom Sohan Singh described as "a killer" who died in the "heat of battle." This apology showed the "moral courage" of the militants, Sohan Singh said.[26]

Though Sohan Singh showed little reservation about the way that the militants used their force, Simranjit Singh Mann was more reflective. Although he had no moral qualms about Sikhs destroying those considered to be enemies of the faith, he felt that there were strategic choices to be made. Like Zaffarwal, Mann made a distinction between "random killing" and "targeted killing." The former, he said, simply scared the general population and made it vulnerable to the potential for even more terror from the state in reprisal. Targeted killing, on the other hand, could broaden the base of support for the movement by inviting sympathy and eliminating ruthless persons. The assassination of Beant Singh was an effective example of targeted killing, Mann said, since he was a symbol of the state's tyranny. Punjab's former police chief, K. P. S. Gill, was a similar symbol. If he were to be killed, it would also be a symbolic act. It would indicate the collective judgment of the Sikhs and the continuing power of the movement.

Surjit Singh: A View From Below

Few of the killings attributed to the various groups associated with the Sikh uprising of the 1980s were conducted by the leaders. Instead the foot soldiers of the movement were called in to do what was described to them as their duty to their community. I talked with a number of these former militants. Perhaps none was more poignant than the story of Surjit Singh.[27]

When I talked with Surjit Singh in the dusty village of Sultanwind several miles outside the Punjab city of Amritsar, he was still bitter. He felt he had been abandoned and misled during the final years during the collapse of the movement and the end of the violence in the 1990s. But when he recalled his earlier experiences during the glory days of the movement, his face began to come alive. Clearly those were the most significant years in his life. "Those were the days," the old rebel told me.[28]

Part of the reason that Surjit Singh was drawn to the movement was a matter of geography. The village of Sultanwind where he was raised and had lived most of his life came to be known as "little Khalistan" since it was in the center of the maelstrom of militant activity. For over ten years the Indian government and its armed police battled against the militant rebels who were led by several organizations structured as military units. All of the young men in his generation were involved in the struggle, Surjit Singh told me. More important, his older brother was a rising star in the movement, and his buddies looked up to him as if he were a football hero. His brother joined one of the central organizations in the militant movement and Surjit looked on with admiration.

Though he was still a teenager, Surjit began joining his brother in some of the nonviolent aspects of the movement. They helped to sponsor a protest march against what they felt was Pakistan's unfair exploitation of water from the Sutlej River, which deprived Sikh farmers in the Indian Punjab of their full allotment. In the early 1980s the older brother began spending time listening to the teachings of Jarnail Singh Bhindranwale, the key figure in the Khalistan movement, and spreading his message of the unity of rural Sikhs—mostly from the landowning Jat community—in opposition to what he described as the oppression of the Indian government.

Surjit Singh realized that his older brother was secretly occupied with suspicious activities, but he claimed that he was unaware of the details. The Punjab police, however, assumed that both brothers were involved in nefarious activities and arrested Surjit along with his brother, though only for brief periods of time since they did not have firm evidence against them. In 1986, the police arrested the elder brother again, and according to Surjit Singh they tortured his brother for a month before putting him to death in an extrajudicial execution. The police began to target Surjit Singh as well, assuming he was also culpable in whatever crimes they suspected his brother of committing. Surjit Singh went into hiding. Later that year, when he was twenty-one years old, he became fully committed to the movement. He joined a rebel group that was prominent in Sultanwind, and spent the next six years as a militant, moving from village to village under cover of night to avoid detection by the police.

Eventually he was captured. By then it was the 1990s, when the movement was falling apart. Villagers were no longer willing to shelter the militant groups, and the Punjab police were rounding up anyone who might be a suspect, dead or alive. Surjit Singh was brought in alive, and for the next eight years waited in prison for one trial after another. He was accused of having been a hit man who killed police, informants, and their families on behalf of the militant movements. The evidence, however, was deemed insufficient for conviction, and eventually Surjit Singh was released. His life since then, however, has been restricted. His passport was taken away, so he cannot travel outside the country; he is unable to receive government loans or benefits; and he is under continued surveillance.

When I asked him why he had joined the movement in the first place, he hesitated before answering. The police treated him as the enemy, he said, so he reacted in kind. He added that he thought he was doing something good for his community. Besides, everyone was joining the movement in those days, and he wanted to impress his brother. There was silence, as if he was looking for some other, more basic, explanation. "It was what we did," he finally said, as if there were no other option.

This was a typical response, I was told by my colleague Jagrup Singh Sekhon. "They were just caught up in the moment," he said.[29] Sekhon, a political scientist, was not just speaking from vague observation; he and two other social scientists at Guru Nanak Dev University had interviewed hundreds of people in the Punjab in an effort to understand who the militants were and what their motives might have been.

The results of this study were published as *Terrorism in Punjab: Understanding Grassroots Reality.*[30] The scholars and their research teams went to twenty-eight locations in the heart of Amritsar district, where they interviewed the families and other villagers knowledgable about 323 militants. They interviewed very few former militants, in part because they estimated that 79 percent of them had been killed in battle, and those who survived often did not want to be identified with the movement for fear of police reprisal. Their families and other villagers, on the other hand, had little to lose, and after gaining their confidence the scholars were able to secure fairly open responses.

One of the main findings of the research project had to do with the motives of the militants—the so-called "boys" whose average age was twenty-two. In an open-ended question about why the boys joined the movement, over twenty disparate answers were given, ranging from economic opportunism to revenge against police brutality. The largest response, however, was simply "for fun." Almost 40 percent said that the excitement and thrill of being engaged in a great battle was the key motivation. Another 12 percent said that the lads hoped to make money though the gang's smuggling and looting operations, 11 percent said they were influenced by other people in the movement and wanted to join them, and only 5 percent said their main motivation was to create a Sikh state, a Khalistan.[31]

Interestingly, 90 percent of the militants in this survey joined after 1986, during one of the highest periods of violence. This would correspond to the attraction of the thrill of battle, since the boys would have witnessed the maelstrom following the army's attack on the Golden Temple in Operation Blue Star. They saw signs of dangerous activity all around them and were eager to join in. The study is one snapshot in time, however, and it would be interesting to see if the responses would have been different if they were able to interview people related to militants in the early years of the movement. The survey also did not record whether there were changes in the militants' attitudes as their involvement continued. As I mentioned, Zaffarwal said he initially joined because of police harassment, but later accepted as a key idea that they were fighting for faith and Khalistan. Almost none of the militants surveyed by Puri, Judge, and Sekhon, however, were said to be noticeably religious; scarcely 5 percent knew anything about the Sikh scriptures.[32] Other observers claim that the respondents to the survey deliberately masked the true intentions of the activists, and that they were more committed than they might have appeared to be.

Whatever the case, the militants were not casual participants. Like the cadres that flocked to Iraq and Syria to fight for the Islamic State, they had cut themselves off from their families. They lived in swarms of guerrilla cells that moved from village to village, finding an *adda* ("station") where they could stay for a night or two. Often these stations were pre-selected as ones where the villagers were either compliant or intimidated into submission, and where the young men could find food, shelter, and perhaps sexual favors from the young women in the village. Thus they existed in worlds of their own, with an ethics forged out of necessity. The prime virtue was loyalty to their leaders and their groups. The greatest sin was complicity with the police. Violence was accepted as a way of life. Most of the participants showed little remorse for the acts that they committed, even the practice of "chopping into pieces" the bodies of someone they suspected of being a police agent or having cheated on one of the other militants, even if it was simply someone stealing their girlfriend. In one case a schoolteacher riding a bicycle was gunned down, not because the militants had any animosity towards him but simply to impress the nearby villagers and intimidate them into complying with their demands for hospitality.[33]

Thomas Hegghammer, the Norwegian expert on the Islamic State, has written about that movement's culture of violence.[34] He argues that many in the movement were attracted not by the ideology or the ideals, but by the excitement of being involved in an alternative culture, one of largely male militancy. What the study by Sekhon and his colleagues indicates is that the same dynamic was a major part of the attraction for the many young men who joined the Sikh uprising in the 1980s. This is essentially what Surjit Singh told me in his attempt to try to understand why he had joined the movement. In his telling it seemed that he did not come to the war as much as the war came to him. The sense of struggle, the war world-view, descended on Sultanwind and other Punjab villages at the time like a dark cloud, engulfing everything. Without quite wanting or asking for it, they were at war.

K.P.S. Gill and the End of Khalistan

Eventually wars end. The Sikh militant uprising began to unravel in the early 1990s. There were a variety of factors involved in its demise, though one man is often given the lion's share of the credit: Kanwar Pal Singh Gill. He was Director General of Police in the Punjab during two crucial periods of the uprising, 1988–1990 and 1991–1994. It was during his second tour of duty as DG of Police that the movement came to an end, and perhaps no one has given K.P.S. Gill more credit for that than Gill himself.

With the help of some friends in Delhi I had traced Gill's location to the Hindu pilgrimage town of Vrindavan, midway between Delhi and Agra on the banks of the Jumna river. It was a place where Gill often stayed, at a former palace at Keshi Ghat owned by Chandi Heffner, an American woman who was one of the recipients of the estate of Tobacco Company heiress Doris Duke. Heffner was with Gill when I met with them in the living room of the slightly crumbling palace, where Gill was wrapped in blankets next to an old-fashioned coil heater. In the background a television set was turned to CNN's live coverage of the inauguration of Donald Trump. Gill was a huge fan of Trump, he said, admiring his bold style and braggadocio. He lamented that they could not get Fox News in India and instead had to rely on the international coverage of CNN.[35]

Though coughing and a bit frail, Gill still had a strong sturdy voice and an unwavering conviction that all of his actions throughout his life had been correct. He was pleased, he said, to have earned the nickname of India's "super cop." When I met with him he was surrounded by an armed guard, but he did not seem concerned about threats on his life. As I mentioned earlier, the

Khalistan leader Simranjit Singh Mann had said that the assassination of Gill, like that of Punjab's chief minister Beant Singh, would be greeted with applause from the Sikh community. Another former leader of the militant movement, Major General Narinder Singh, agreed that Beant Singh "had to be killed," and that Gill would be targeted soon—"tomorrow," as he put it.[36] Gill dismissed these statements as the pompous rantings of popularist politicians. Gill in fact died four months after my conversation with him, though of natural causes, at the age of eighty-two.

When I talked with him, Gill had no regrets. He told me that the whole lot of insurgents, from the young Sikh militants to their older, manipulative leaders, should have been locked up or eliminated from the very beginning. Indeed many have said that this was Gill's strategy: simply killing off the militants. I asked whether the movement might have been weakened from within as well as through the massive police effort that he commanded at the time, since the militants' stance had degenerated from one of high-minded religious causes to a kind of thuggery. "They were always thugs," Gill said, "and deserved to be treated as such."[37] He showed little remorse for the many lives that were lost in what the government often described as "police encounters," implying that this loss of life was necessary to secure public order.

In his final assault on the militants in the early 1990s, Gill launched a massive police action. Central to his counterterrorism strategy was a military-style take-no-prisoners approach to rounding up young men suspected of being supporters. He is said to have given his police officers a bounty on the heads of militants that they were able to kill. He eschewed the idea that they should be taken as prisoners, who would then quarrel with the government in lengthy court cases. He equipped his police force with military-style weapons and equipment. In my conversation with Gill, he was proud that he had earned a reputation for the "Gill doctrine" in defeating terrorism, and as a result had served as a consultant for countries as diverse as Sri Lanka and Afghanistan on how to deal with terrorists. When I asked him to define the Gill doctrine, he said it was simple: "go for the leaders and go after the weapons."[38] He denied that any of the militants had altruistic motives. He thought that the youth were attracted to the movement only for one purpose: to get their hands on a gun.

Despite Gill's conviction that his approach was responsible for the end of the movement, it should be noted that in the first year of his all-out assault on the movement the number of deaths attributed to the militants actually rose to over six thousand, the largest number killed in a single year over the entire history of the uprising. Thus the initial response to his approach was to make matters worse. Whether the diminishment of the movement in subsequent years was due solely or even largely to his take-no-prisoners efforts is not clear. The other thing that was happening at the time was a decay of organization and idealism within the movement itself.

Most of those whom I interviewed who were closely involved in the movement as leaders or observers attributed the decline of the movement to the in-fighting within it, and the collapse of a sense of noble purpose. The "boys" were no longer fighting for a Sikh cause. "They ended up like street gangs," the old militant, Narinder Singh, said about the fighters in the last years of the movement.[39] He said that they were only interested in power and extorting villagers for support, including sexual favors that were demanded from the women in the villages. Needless to say, this did not endear the villagers to them. The safe shelter that they had come to expect from the rural areas began to erode. The high-minded image of cosmic war as a battle between right and wrong, truth and evil, became hard to maintain in the messy squabbles of youth gangs seeking power, money, and sex.

In explaining the years of terror visited on the Punjab, the former militant leader, Narinder Singh, concluded that sometimes "the boys"—as the Sikh militants were commonly called—"were hot-headed." It was this passion that was their eventual undoing. "Eventually the people became sick of all the killings," he explained in accounting for why the movement came to an end. Someday, he added, the movement will rise again. But not now, he said. "All the boys are dead."[40]

After the movement was largely over, many of the former leaders who had survived the police onslaught were put on trial, but few were convicted, since the evidence of their criminality was lacking. Some were lured into the political area. In an effort to put the past behind it, the government also chose to give amnesty to leaders such as Simranjit Singh Mann, who turned his attention to running for political office. Wassan Singh Zaffarwal, among others, emerged from the shadows to face court trials but then resumed normal lives. One of the earliest ideologues in the movement, Dr. Jagjit Singh Chohan, returned to the Punjab from London in 2001 after twenty-five years in exile. He set up a charitable hospital and established an unsuccessful political party that continued to advocate for Khalistan.[41] One of the leaders of the movement's Akal Federation, Bhai Kanwar Singh Dhami, after serving a prison sentence, proclaimed that the "movement is dead" and then established a trust administering orphanages for children of slain militants and financial support for their widows.[42] Virsa Singh Valtoha, a known militant, spent years in jail and then emerged to become an MLA (member of the Punjab legislative assembly) for the Akali Party.[43]

The Indian government also reached out to Sikhs who had not been involved in the uprising to demonstrate that their religious community was a vital part of the Indian nation. The internationally famous economist Manmohan Singh, a Sikh—though one who had no part in the insurrection—was made Prime Minister of India by the Congress Party, thus elevating the visibility of the Sikh religion to the national stage. The Punjab government also provided funds to improve Sikh shrines, including a massive reconstruction of the urban area around the central Sikh pilgrimage site and former battleground, the Golden Temple, where the government created a kind of Disneyland mall to attract visitors and provide modern amenities for pilgrims to the area. In these ways the government tried to provide the respect that many Sikhs felt they had not previously received.

The image of war dissipated both because some of the causes of discontent were met, and because the image itself was no longer viable. The army of militants turned out to be less than worthy stewards of the high vision of Khalistan, and the possibilities of any kind of victory against the strong defense of Gill's militarized police force seemed increasingly unlikely. By 1995 the war was over. Life in the villages returned to normal.

The lure of Khalistan is still in the air, however. In the first decades of the century, voices from within Punjab and among the expatriate community in the United Kingdom, the United States, and Canada were heard again urging a new Khalistan movement. In London in 2019 Sikhs protesting at the venue of the Cricket World Cup events raised Khalistan slogans. In India, the resentment over Gill's militant repression left a bitterness among many former Sikh leaders that has not diminished, and there was again a sense of economic despair in the Punjab countryside that has led to political protest. Sikh farmers, the community from which the Khalistan movement had sprung, were among the most strident supporters of the 2020–21 Indian farmers protest movement that fought against the central government's new agricultural legislation. Some media reports claimed that Khalistan advocates had infiltrated the protests in Delhi, New York City, and elsewhere.[44] Sikh activism, for two decades thought to be dead, showed new signs of life. But the state of Punjab was at peace. The insurrection of the 1980s has faded into the past.

When I asked the old militant leader, Wassan Singh Zaffarwal, at what moment he realized that the uprising was finally over, he thought for a while before answering. At first he mentioned his awareness of the in-fighting within the movement, and the disorganization and lack of command chains that allowed gangs of militants to turn into thugs. He also mentioned the police violence and intimidation in their final surge of repression against the movement. But then he paused and said that it was the villagers who made the difference. "When they turned against us," he said, "we knew it was over."[45]

5   *How Imagined Wars End*

When Wassan Singh Zaffarwal told me that he knew the movement was over when villagers stopped supporting it, the sad resignation in his voice was palpable.[1] It was echoed in the comments from the former militants in the other two movements that I have studied for this project. The ex-jihadi in Iraq, Muhammad, complained bitterly that the leaders had let the movement down, attributing the erosion of the movement and its vulnerability to outside destruction to their lack of dedication, but his commitment to the ideals of the movement were not over. Naguib Sinarimbo in Mindanao thought that it was inevitable that the war mentality would be challenged by the reality that they could not win by violent means, and they needed to adapt; now they had to adjust to a post-war world.[2]

In each case there was a sadness in the voices of each of these old activists, a sense that they had lost a part of themselves in the ending of their militant movements. They remembered the excitement and challenge of being called to a great cause. And now they had to reconcile themselves to a different situation, where militancy was no longer a possibility.

Nonetheless, though there are similarities in the way in which these former combatants viewed their past participation in the movement, each movement ended somewhat differently. And in each case there are multiple dimensions to the way in which the fighting terminated.

The three case studies in this book reveal the complexity of how imagined wars come to an end. In describing each of them—the collapse of ISIS, the termination of the Khalistan movement in India's Punjab, and the attempts to settle the ongoing insurgency in the Philippines aimed at creating a Muslim Mindanao region—I have tried to understand how conflict is resolved not only when armed fighting ceases, but also when the idea of conflict itself dissipates. I wanted to know whether the gripping notion of cosmic war disappears, or whether it is sustained in some other form and the adherents simply accommodate themselves to the reality of a changed situation. What I have found is that both things are true, related to structural changes within and outside the movements.

There are both external and internal factors to the way a movement ends. Externally, the limitations on a movement (including military action and destruction of its bases) help to jar participants' acceptance of the futility of waging war. But there are also internal disagreement and changes in perception that are equally, if not more, important. Some movements are essentially dead before they are destroyed. There are different ways in which this can happen—the compelling image of cosmic war can degenerate into internecine warfare, or followers may be co-opted into non-militant politics.

Each of the cases I have examined here follow different trajectories, and in two of them—ISIS and the Mindanao movement—the militancy limps on in a truncated fashion, while in the third, the Sikh case, sparks of revival have flared up because the situation was never fully resolved. In Mindanao, the image of war was episodic, depending on whether a peaceful outcome of the struggle was deemed to be possible. In Khalistan, though all-encompassing during the height of the movement, the worldview of warfare dissipated over time. In the case of ISIS, among the true believers the idea of cosmic battle survived as a vision for the future while most of its adherents adjusted to new realities.

Under what conditions do images of imagined war end? This is an interesting question not only from the point of view of social movement analysis, but from a policy perspective as well. The answer to the question may cause policymakers to alter how they try to deal with movements that are swept up in visions of cosmic war.

I am aware that I am not the first person to try to understand how such movements terminate, and that other scholars have provided useful studies. One of the most comprehensive is Audrey Kurth Cronin's *How Terrorism Ends*.[3] In this book, Cronin surveys dozens of cases and organizes them into six ways in which movements end: through the decapitation of the leaders, negotiation, achieving their objective, imploding, repression, and reorientation to nonviolent activities. Another useful study is Isak Svensson's *Ending Holy Wars: Religion and Conflict Resolution in Civil Wars.* In it Svensson probes the religious factor in rebel movements and analyzes how it complicates and sometimes helps the process of negotiated settlement.[4] These and other books provide helpful distinctions, though my approach is somewhat different. I want to understand how the collapse of movements is perceived from the perspective of those who are engaged in them, and to ask how the image of grand warfare that animates them is eventually discarded, or distanced from their current realities.

The three case studies that I have reviewed in this essay give several possible answers. One is that these images might retreat on their own. The image of cosmic war is a fantastic one, and as compelling as it may be for an intense period of time within an inner circle, it may never have been a dominant theme for many of the foot soldiers. Even for the true believers the idea of ordinary war might simply have vanished as time went on and no measurable gains were seen, and as individuals at the margins of the movement drifted off to other things. This is in part what happened in the Punjab case, though the police authorities were convinced their own overwhelming force obliterated the movement. In this instance, as with the Mindanao and ISIS cases, the actions of the government, through peaceful negotiation on the one hand and strong military action on the other, indeed played a role in the degradation of the movements and the collapse of the image of war. But it was not the only factor, and not necessarily the most important one.

To understand how this process happens, how the idea of imagined war dissipates, we have to take both internal and external perspectives into account. Through interviews and examining reports of the activities within the movements, I have tried to gain insights on what internal factors were critical in the collapse of the image of war. Similarly, I have tried to understand how the movements' opposition—government authorities, in most cases—has played a role in this demise, and what other external factors have been critical as well.

Internal Conditions

In my conversation with the former jihadi militant, Muhammad, he seemed even angrier about the failed leadership of the ISIS and al-Qaeda movements than he was about the combined Iraqi, Syrian, Kurdish and United States forces that were united against them. It was the leadership, Muhammad groused, that let the movement down. Not only did it discredit the organization, it did disservice to the grand image of the Caliphate and the great war for which he thought there was a divine mandate. In his mind the movement was dead before it was demolished.

Some of the same feelings were expressed by Surjit Singh and other Khalistan foot soldiers. Though the leaders with whom I spoke, including Wassan Singh Zaffarwal, Sohan Singh, Simranjit Singh Mann, and Narinder Singh, were hesitant to blame themselves or their fellow leaders, they admitted that internal divisions and loss of vision contributed to the movement's downfall. In Mindanao, the old militants blamed the schisms in the movement for part of their ineffectiveness, but they also said that another internal factor was the awareness of possibilities of success outside the revolutionary strategies that they had previously adopted.

These internal factors can be clustered into three categories: a loss of faith in the movement's vision, fractures in the communal consensus of the organization, and the awareness of alternative opportunities that provide new hope.

Loss of Faith

In a refugee camp near Mosul in Northern Iraq, I talked with a wife of a former ISIS militant who openly displayed her disdain towards the movement and what it had done to her husband. She claimed that it had ruined her family's life. She did not know where her husband was, whether he was dead or alive, and—if alive—whether he was awaiting trial or even execution. It was all a maddening mystery to her. She said she had once believed in the Caliphate, but now it seemed like an empty hoax.

Though I found that not all former fighters and their supporters felt this way, I knew that many did. But when did their faith in the Caliphate and its notion of cosmic war begin to erode? I put this question to the wife of the former militant and at first she did not give an answer. When pressed, she muttered, "when things fell apart."

This answer was consistent with other accounts that I heard from former ISIS supporters, and from reports from other scholars and journalists who have interviewed them. When things were going well, when the Caliphate was expanding and the stolen resources from the region were sufficient to provide for the necessities in life, it was easy to believe in the prophetic future of a golden era that would be ushered in after this period of turmoil. But later, as their homes were destroyed and the movement was falling apart, it all seemed like a cruel joke.

In the Khalistan movement in India, several of the ex-militants with whom I spoke said that the movement began to collapse when it no longer had purpose. There was a moment, they said, when their organizations were fighting for Khalistan and for the dignity of Sikhs as a community. But later they saw the movement degenerate into infighting and thuggery. Though the research by the social scientists at Guru Nanak Dev University in Amritsar cast doubt on how much the ordinary youths in the later years of the movement were ever motivated by the high ideals that the leaders espoused, there is no question that some, especially in the early years, at least gave lip service to that higher vision.[5] For them the excitement of being part of a thrilling battle was enhanced by the sense that they were in a war for their faith, fighting for all that was right and sacred, a war propelled by divine forces. As the movement slid into drug-dealing and petty theft, it was hard to maintain that lofty image.

In the Philippines, the evolution of Abu Sayyaf is further testimony to the dissolution of a movement's ideals. One of the founders of the movement, Abdurajik Abubakar Janjalani, had been a teacher of Islamic theology and had been involved in the mujahidin militia in Afghanistan. One of the reasons that he broke from the Moro National Liberation Front was because of religion. He thought that the MNLF had abandoned its lofty religious ideals and was pandering to political expediency in negotiations with the Philippine government. He wanted his movement to be more pure in its intentions, and to engage in jihad with a spiritual as well as political purpose. Over time, however, Abu Sayyaf became identified with drug dealing and taking hostages for profit. In proclaiming itself affiliated with the Islamic State it attempted to regain its religious credibility, though other Muslim activists with whom I talked in Mindanao regarded its religiosity as a front for what had essentially become a criminal gang.

In each of these cases the character of the movement changed when the vision was abandoned. Even though the fighting continued, as it did in the case of Khalistan and Abu Sayyaf's branch of the Moro movement, there was a change in the way that the movement was seen by its members. Surjit Singh told me that after a while he did not know why they were fighting, except to sustain themselves through stolen resources. He indicated that he would have left the militant Sikh moment earlier than he did, but he did not know how to do so. He was afraid that the police would not trust him and he would be finished off in a "police encounter," the term often used for extrajudicial killings. Or, if he showed weakness and an eagerness to leave, he feared that members of the movement would turn on him and extinguish him in an effort to prevent any information about the movement's location and activities from leaking out. Despite these fears, many supporters at the margins of the movement were able to simply fade into the background as it declined. Weary of terror and war, fringe members began to drop off.

Fractures in Communal Consensus

At the same time that they lost faith in the purpose of the movement, many militants were disillusioned by infighting within their organization. Muhammad told me about a disagreement that he had with a fellow jihadi over strategy, a fight that turned violent. Muhammad pulled up his shirt to show me the scar from where he had been stabbed in the encounter. Increasingly, it had seemed to him that they were fighting as much among themselves as they were against their perceived enemies.

The ISIS movement remained intact even though there was fighting within the ranks. In the case of the Khalistan and Moro movements, however, the infighting led to multiplying schisms. When I interviewed the old Khalistan leader, Wassan Singh Zaffarwal, he expressed frustration that his attempt to unite all of the different rebel movements under the umbrella of a Panthic Committee was not successful. The Babbar Khalsa never joined the committee, and the Bhindranwale Tiger Force joined it briefly before breaking off on their own. Even Zaffarwal's own organization, the Khalistan Commando Force, broke into several quarreling camps.

Sometimes the divisions between these splinter movements could turn deadly. In the Khalistan movement, the numbers of Sikhs killed by Sikh militants increased dramatically over the years that the movement was active.[6] Infighting may have led indirectly to the military invasion that resulted in Bhindranwale's death. A former member of the inner circle of the movement was bribed by a rival faction to kill Bhindranwale, or failing that, to do in his right-hand man, Surinder Singh Sodhi, a young admirer of Bhindranwale whom the leader called "my brother."[7] The killers gunned down Sodhi in a tea stall, after which Bhindranwale lashed out at his rivals for what he described as "chopping my right hand."[8] In revenge for the killing his henchmen murdered several key personnel in the rival movement, thus prompting the Indian army to step up its plans to invade the Golden Temple, which took place soon after.

In the Moro movement, the emergence of a splinter group, the Bangsamoro Islamic Freedom Fighters, was aimed in part at discrediting the negotiating tactics of the main movement in central Mindanao, the Moro Islamic Liberation Front. Butch Malang, the commander of the MILF forces, told me that although some of his own fighters had joined the breakaway movement, the lives of the MILF fighters were put in jeopardy by the splinter group's actions. Many of Malang's group felt that their lives were threatened as much by BIFF as by the Philippine government forces.

Part of the reason for the divisions within the Moro movement was that there was never a centralized command, nor a single leader. In the case of the Khalistan movement, the figure of Bhindranwale provided something of a unifying image of leadership for the movement, despite the rival organizations that emerged in the Sikh resistance. After Bhindranwale was killed in Operation Blue Star in 1984, however, the movement failed to find another charismatic figure to unite it. Later in the 1980s even the parallel organizations, such as the Khalistan Commando Force and the Sikh Students Federation, broke apart into splinter organizations that vied with each other for attention and support. In the case of ISIS, the figure of the Caliph, Abu Bakr al-Baghdadi, provided the central leadership that largely united the movement. But the organizational structure was generally decentralized, and on the local level there were the fierce battles for leadership and strident infighting which Muhammad found so disheartening.

Though Muhammad clung to the idea of a Caliph as a righteous ruler worth fighting for, he seemed uncertain about whether al-Baghdadi was a sufficiently strong leader to deserve that title. According to the Islamic studies scholar Ebrahim Moosa, a Caliph can lose his divine mandate when he is regarded as not performing like a Caliph.[9] It is not clear whether this is the way that many of the ISIS fighters viewed al-Baghdadi, especially during the last days of the territorial control of the movement, but Muhammad was clear in his blame of the movement's leadership without specifying whom he had in mind.

Faith in a movement can erode when its leader is seen as less than legitimate. It could be through demonstrations of their incompetence, greed, or inconsistencies. In the Taliban movement in Afghanistan, the leader Muhammed Omar was said to have lost support from some of his followers when it was revealed that he was living in relative luxury in palatial quarters funded in part by Osama bin Laden. Posthumous respect for bin Laden was said to have diminished when it was revealed that a stash of pornographic videotapes was found in his quarters when the hideout was invaded by American soldiers in the attack that led to bin Laden's death.

The death of a leader does not necessarily lead to a loss of regard for his authority. In the case of the Palestinian resistance in Israel, the Israeli missile attack that destroyed Hamas leader Sheikh Ahmed Yassin was not the occasion for his image to lose credibility or the movement to erode. Just the opposite. He was immediately proclaimed a martyr, and pictures of the fallen leader were plastered throughout the region. The elections following his death led to overwhelming support for Hamas and the establishment of Hamas control in Gaza. In the case of ISIS, the death of al-Baghdadi in 2019 during an American military raid on his quarters in the Idlib region of Syria did not signal the end of the Caliphate, or a lack of respect for the fallen leader's image. For one thing, he committed suicide as the troops encircled him, thereby dying through self-martyrdom, an appropriate end for a jihadi leader. Moreover his successor was quickly named, and the ideas of a Caliphate and an Islamic State endured. As in the case of Hamas, movements can sometimes become stronger after a charismatic leader is killed and the fallen leader is treated as a martyr. Although Bhindranwale's movement splintered organizationally, the number of young people who volunteered to join the movement increased after his death in 1984. They were in part inspired by his legendary martyrdom.

When a movement is already weak and its authority is challenged, the killing of a leader can help to hasten a movement's demise. This may be what has happened with Abu Sayyaf and the Maute brothers' gang after their leaders were killed in the Marawi siege in Mindanao in 2017. But in this case their groups were already weakened and the leaders' authority questioned as the prognosis for the groups' success diminished in the fighting.

In all three of the cases in my study, the infighting and loss of *esprit de corps* within the movement was a major part of their undoing. When an activist movement divides and turns on itself, the paranoia of the movement turns inwards. The demonization applied to external enemies is turned inward towards perceived heretics, those suspected of treason within their own ranks. Thus, as one old militant said to me, such movements were already "walking dead."

New Hope

There is another powerful internal factor contributing to the transformation of a formerly violent movement: hope. The movement for an autonomous Muslim Mindanao provides an interesting case in this regard. When I asked Naguib Sinarimbo, the ex-Moro militant, to trace the trajectory of his rise within the movement, his full embrace of the image of cosmic war animated by religion and aimed at an intractable enemy, and later his abandonment of this image and an engagement in negotiations for peace, I wanted to know what happened. What was the critical moment in which his views changed?

He said that it was when he met a Philippine general who listened to him. The general seemed genuinely concerned about the plight of the Moro people, and wanted a way out that would give them the dignity for which they sought and the peace that the government demanded. That moment came to Naguib as an epiphany, he said. He did not know that it was possible to see the enemy in such human terms.[10]

It was not just this attitude of respect, he said, it was the larger program that the general and his staff outlined for the Moro people. Naguib was convinced that the agreement that they negotiated really did fulfill the demands that the Moro movement was making, and provided the region with a modicum of independence, economic support, and respect.

Naguib was expressing a vital part of the peace process that leads to an end of conflict. This is when combatants can see beyond war and imagine opportunities for themselves after the fighting is over. Fighting no longer seems desirable or necessary. In the Palestinian movement, the suicide bombings attributed to the Hamas movement declined during times when negotiated peace settlements seemed possible and economic conditions in Gaza and the West Bank improved. They also declined when Hamas was given a political role and its followers perceived that they had a voice in public life. When they felt that their voice was not being listened to, however, either their own followers or a schismatic group would turn to violence again, and the cycle of war would return. In the case of Khalistan it is noteworthy that some of the old Khalistan leaders, including Wassan Singh Zaffarwal, Jagjit Singh Chohan, and Simranjit Singh Mann, turned to electoral politics in the years after the demise of the movement. They were able to see a future role for themselves in public life.

In Mindanao, leaders like Naguib Sinarimbo were also planning for roles in electoral politics. They were getting ready for the next stage of the movement, the implementation of Bangsamoro as a political entity. This meant that the leaders and fighters in an armed struggle over many years had to learn to adjust to peace. They had to treat the government like an ally rather than a foe, and learn the arts of compromise and negotiation that all politicians have to adopt.

This was not an easy task. As Naguib told me, many of his colleagues were skeptical. Some left the movement in dismay over what they regarded as capitulation. Many who were wavering needed reassurances and support. One of the reasons why the transition was so difficult was that it required longtime militants to adopt a radically new view of the world. They were being asked to abandon the vision of a cosmic war between good and evil that had animated much of their struggle, and that made mortal enemies out of those with whom they differed, including the government and other branches of the movement. Butch Malang admitted that was a daunting assignment. It took him a year, he said, to adjust to the new reality, and he did so eventually only with grave misgivings.

"Some of our fighters know only how to fight," he said, somewhat sadly.[11] In his case, however, the old commander eventually took on a new role of facilitator in one of the major aspects of the peace process, the cessation of hostilities. New circumstances—the hope of a settlement—can make veterans look differently at a struggle, and even imagine the possibilities of reconciliation and peace. Moreover, it helps when the government gives roles to their old adversaries and actively promotes a rehabilitation program for former militants, programs that provide networks of social support and training for new jobs outside the military arena. These are attempts to return combatants to ordinary society, to allow them to see a role for themselves outside the struggle.

Religion has played a role in attempts to move from conflict to peace, and in Mindanao it was once a destructive one, buttressing the bellicose jihadi worldview. But religion has also been employed in positive ways in recent years. Since the MILF movement influences all of the mosques in the area, Sinarimbo told me, it has given the imams in each instructions on what to include in their sermons about the peace process. The imams have encouraged the faithful to embrace the plan and not reject it as the BIFF and Abu Sayyaf urged them to do. Hence the most profound change within the movement has been a shift in attitude away from the divisions of the past and towards a different role within society that no longer requires militancy to achieve social change.

External Conditions

How authorities respond to militant movements is vital in how the movements will react. As one jihadi in Iraq told me, his group closely observed everything the government did and said, and acted accordingly. Surjit Singh, along with other old Khalistan activists, said that the actions of the police dictated how the movement would respond, and indeed he and Zaffarwal credited the growth of the movement to young people's animosity against what they regarded as heavy-handed police repression.

Given that any attempt by the authorities to suppress a movement might backfire and create greater violence in response, should authorities do nothing at all? That is indeed a legitimate question, since one could adopt a "wait and see" attitude and assume that a movement will collapse by itself, as is eventually often the case. It may not be a bad strategy, since what authorities frequently do—engage in militarized overreactions to terrorism—can actually make matters worse. So in some cases they might have been better off having done nothing at all. If the Indian army had not invaded the Golden Temple in Operation Blue Star, for instance, it is conceivable that the Sikh insurrection would have died out much earlier than it did. Yet the Punjab movement had lasted for years before that attack, which is a long time to sustain the idea of cosmic war, and a long time for a populace to be terrorized by a movement. Similarly, the terror and torture unleashed by the Islamic State in the three years of its heyday could not be tolerated for long. In such situations authorities have felt compelled to do something.

What they do, however, can have a significant impact on whether the movement and its image of cosmic war thrives or shrinks away. As I mentioned, a movement of opposition to an authority is always highly conscious of what the authority does. How the authorities respond to terrorism and the vision of war that propels it will determine how the movement thinks of itself and its relationship to the worldview of the larger society in which it exists. From the case studies that I have examined, the following appear to be essential elements in formulating policies that are effective in bringing a vision of cosmic war to an end.

Strong Limitations

The main danger of doing nothing, as I suggested above, is not just that it allows a movement to maintain its reign of violence. The absence of strong authoritative control gives a movement the illusion that it can do whatever it wants, and that there are no limitations on its authority.

This was the disaster that occurred in the military triumph of the Islamic State. When its forces rolled over eastern Syria and western Iraq, it found little credible resistance. The Syrian army was virtually absent and the Iraqi army crumbled like a house of cards. One could imagine that a more secure political structure would have had the police and military strength to prohibit ISIS from gaining the foothold that allowed it to create, for a time, its own imaginary kingdom. Yet the use of military force is a delicate matter.

In my previous writings on how authorities should respond to religious-based terrorist movements, I have warned against the excessive use of force, especially military force, since that can reinforce the rebels' worldview that they are engaged in a cosmic war. It often makes the situation worse, and brings more terrorism in its wake. In each of these cases, there is ample evidence that this is indeed the case, from Philippine military attacks on Moro protestors to Operation Blue Star in India that led to a renewed vibrancy of the Sikh separatist movement. Though K. P. S Gill thinks that his own strong-armed police tactics destroyed the Khalistan movement when he was in charge from 1991 to 1995, it is also true that when he led the government forces in an earlier assignment to Punjab, from 1988 to 1990, the terrorist movement grew, and even during the final period initially there were more deaths than at any earlier point in the movement's history.

As evidence of his success, Gill told me that his leadership in another attack on militants in the Golden Temple following the 1984 Operation Blue Star fiasco demonstrated the efficacy of strategic military action. In 1988 militants again occupied the precincts of the Golden Temple, thinking it was a safe haven. This time, however, Gill was in charge of the police force. He used a more limited cadre in a targeted action called Operation Black Thunder that killed militants without destroying buildings in the Golden Temple quarters or killing innocent pilgrims to the sacred shrine. Gill takes credit for having depleted the forces of the militants in this operation. Yet a written report found on the body of one of the militants killed at the time, Labh Singh, a general in the Khalistan Commando Force, tells a somewhat different story. The unsigned eight-page report assesses the strength of the movement shortly before the police operation and states that the militants were in serious trouble due to the erosion of support from the villagers in the Punjab who were "alienated by the extortion of money, indiscriminate killings, and other anti-social activities."[12]

Despite Gill's attempt to take credit for destroying the movement, the assessment of the leaders of the movement was that they were already in serious trouble. As Labh Singh's report and Wassan Singh Zaffarwal's comments to me have indicated, the demise of popular support had doomed the militant movement well before the police finished it off. It is quite likely that it would have dissipated on its own, even without Gill's strong-arm tactics. But perhaps the uprising would not have ended as quickly or as decisively without police suppression. Though the evidence from the perspective of the militants is that their movement had already decayed from within and Gill simply performed the *coup de grace,* it could be argued that even if this was the case it was a useful military intervention. Without some kind of firm action, remnants of the movement might have lingered on for years, terrorizing villages.

The time for police action is not just at the end of a movement's career, however, but more importantly at the beginning. If there had been a stronger and more respected police presence in the rural areas of the Punjab it might have deterred the rebels from gaining control of the countryside at the outset.

At various moments in the attempts to contain a violent movement, then, there is a useful role for armed force, including police and even, at times, military units. In the three cases that I have examined in this book, one of the primary actions of authorities was to contain the notion of war, limit those who viewed the world at war from acting out on their bellicose intentions, and restore civil order. This is where police action and military operations have been or should have been involved. Part of the reason for this is to protect lives, and to keep planned violence from being implemented. Obviously the security of the public is a paramount goal of any governmental authority.

But there is another reason why the forceful set of limitations by authorities through police and military units is important: they provide a reality check on an imagined war. They show that this worldview is not acceptable outside the narrow confines of the group that has a vision of cosmic war. The task of a police or military force is to impose a situation of civil order as a viable option to the state of war that a violent movement requires. This means stopping violence in progress, and bringing those who have committed offenses to justice.

When police or military force is applied it is vital that it follow the rule of law. Miscreants should be brought to justice, evidence presented, and judgement rendered. The value of this approach is that it reinforces the notion that civil society should be respected and that the insurgent forces are the lawless ones. In attempting to quash the Sikh separatist movement in the Punjab, K.P.S. Gill adopted tactics that turned many against the police. In addition to paying bounties to his own police squads when they literally brought in the heads of those said to be terrorists, he also paid similar bounties to the "cats," as he called them, former militants who were bribed to be turncoats. Many of these cats used their power indiscriminately, falsely accusing people in order to receive the financial rewards for revealing them.[13] Many Sikhs in the Punjab continue to resent the police for this reason. Similarly, Mindanao residents were revolted by the destruction of the city of Marawi in the army's attempt to capture the militants hiding there, just as the Sunni Arabs in Syria and Iraq were dismayed to see their cities of Raqqa and Mosul destroyed.

Extrajudicial killings by police and overwhelming military assaults on rebel strongholds often presented those who witnessed them, the bystanders in villages and towns that were under siege, with the impression that it was the authorities, not the insurgents, who were lawless. Such tactics appeared to be police terrorism, and buttressed support for the rebels who required the tacit support of the general population in order to thrive. The old guerrilla analogy of fish needing the water of popular support applies.

But, as I say, a strong police presence is often necessary, especially at the outset of a rebellion, to maintain the rule of law. In each of the cases that I examined, the absence of firm limitations in the initial stages of the movements allowed them to grow. In the case of the Punjab, the lack of village-level authority allowed the young militants to do anything they wanted, virtually unchecked. They were able to seize whole sections of the countryside and set up their own alternative rule, especially at night when the Punjab police left and the militants took control of the villages. In Mindanao, a similar lawlessness on the village level allowed the more militant Moro activists to develop a cosmic-war ideology without being challenged by an alternative view of civil order. And in western Iraq and eastern Syria, virtual anarchy reigned in the period after, respectively, the withdrawal of US troops and the rise of the Arab Spring protests in 2011, giving ample room for a revived al-Qaeda in Iraq to morph into the Islamic State with its imagined apocalyptic scenario of cosmic war.

In each of these cases firm police presence and in some cases military resistance was appropriate to hold the movements in check and to demonstrate the limitations of ideas of war. Yet too much military force could fulfill the image of cosmic war rather than contain it. This is what happened in the Punjab in 1984 with the assault on the Golden Temple, and in the Philippines with early attempts of the government to "fight fire with fire" when they overreacted to rebel actions. And in Iraq, the very presence of the United States Army and other collaborating military units was enough to fulfill the image of an enemy that the Islamists in al-Qaeda in Iraq, and later ISIS, wanted to portray.

In each case, however, some authorities learned lessons from these overreactions, and tried to employ military force more strategically. In the Philippines the military eventually stayed on the sidelines as negotiations took place with the militants' leadership and provocations by extreme groups were usually (though not always) ignored, though marginal but violent groups such as Abu Sayyaf were targeted for direct military action. In the Punjab some aspects of the police action led by K. P. S Gill in 1992–1995 were efficacious, such as the effort to send police from local Sikh villages to police their own areas, and to aim for the leadership rather than the general constituencies of support. The police were also employed to help build schools and provide roads in the villages in order to win hearts and minds.[14] In the case of ISIS, the military units that have been used to liberate Fallujah, Ramadi, and Mosul have been a combination of local Sunni militia, Kurdish Peshmerga, and the largely Shi'a Iraqi Army, with the US military playing a supporting role but not visibly prominent. Since the liberating forces were to some degree from the local community, the cosmic-war image of local Muslims versus outsider Americans was not easy to maintain.

It is a difficult balancing act—employing force to limit the spread of a violent movement and provide a reality check on its claims for power while not overreacting in such a way as to validate a notion of cosmic war and provoke more violence in response. Each of these cases show the perils as well as the utility of a measured, strategic use of armed force for peaceful purposes.

Civil Acceptance

Yet authoritative force is effective primarily when it is part of a strategy that responds to the concerns of those who support the rebel forces and provides an alternative view of social order in which those supporters are accepted. Military force by itself is not sufficient to bring about an end to an image of cosmic war. In fact, these three cases that I have examined for this project show that even a small use of armed force can be misconstrued as a hostile act from an evil enemy if it is not accompanied by other efforts of authorities to meet the concerns of the rebels and promote an alternative reality where the militants engaged in the movement can be accepted. This is where measures to provide an accommodation of the movement's goals and the rehabilitation of its militant members are vital.

In some cases it has been possible to negotiate a partial fulfillment of the rebels' goals. In Mindanao, for example, several rounds of negotiations provided for a semiautonomous region of Muslim Mindanao, including the most recent attempt, approved by the Philippine legislature in 2018 and ratified in a Mindanao referendum in 2019. It allows for a degree of political independence and considerable local control of financial matters, including a percentage of tax revenues. As a result, many of the former militant leaders have organized political parties and joined in the electoral process. In Punjab, freedom has been given to some former militants—including two that I have mentioned, the accused mastermind of Indira Gandhi's assassination, Simranjit Singh Mann, and Wassan Singh Zaffarwal, the leader of the guerrilla Khalistan Commando Force. They are now actively engaged in electoral party politics. In Iraq, attempts have been made to ensure that local Sunni leaders will be in charge of the reconstruction of their areas, including Fallujah and Ramadi. In the post-ISIS period much more needs to be done in both Iraq and Syria to ensure that Sunni leaders see themselves as accepted equals in the political life of their countries, rather than untrusted marginal outsiders.

Rehabilitation of soldiers, pardoning and amnesty for militants, and retraining for jobs have been strong elements of the efforts of the Philippine government in Mindanao. In the Punjab there was little attention to providing alternative options for young people, and today the region is wracked with a drug crisis as disillusioned and depressed youth turn to opiates and methamphetamines. In Iraq, the inability of the US-occupied country to find a role for former soldiers in Saddam's huge military was a reason that many of them joined ISIS. Whether the present Iraqi government can find a way to rehabilitate and engage the former ISIS fighters remains to be seen.

Conveying Hope

Perhaps the Philippine army's smartest move in their engagement with the Moro rebels was not a military action, but their choice regarding whom to send as an envoy to negotiate a peace settlement. They designated General Victor Corpus. He was a Philippine army official who had once defected and joined the Communist militants. He later surrendered to the army, was gradually accepted back into the fold and eventually rose to the rank of general. Because of his rebel past, when he met with the Moro rebel leader Naguib Sinarimbo, the general carried the credibility of someone who had been a rebel and then reformed. As I mentioned earlier, General Corpus played a key role in Sinarimbo's acceptance of a peaceful alternative to the Moro struggle.

"He understood us," Naguib said. General Corpus could see how those in the Moro movement would mistrust the government and want to embrace a new way of looking at politics. Yet the general also was realistic. He could explain the futility of guerrilla warfare, and he told Naguib how many of his movement's goals could be met by negotiating a settlement with government officials. Naguib was surprised at how sensitive General Corpus and his colleagues were to the Muslim separatists' concerns. "He respected us," Naguib said.[15]

This is perhaps the most difficult of the approaches that authorities have taken in responding to cases of violent insurgency: conveying an attitude of respect and a message of hope. It is difficult because it requires a change of attitude from the authorities as well as from the militant rebels. In talking with some of the authorities who have been dealing with violent uprisings it is clear that they too have entered into a state of imagined war in treating their opponents as extreme enemies, as less than human. As I reported in the previous chapter, I told Punjab's former police commander, K.P.S. Gill, that many observers thought that in the latter days of the Khalistan movement its own loss of integrity was as much responsible for its collapse as the extrajudicial police "encounters" that led to the deaths of so many of the young militants. "They were always thugs," Gill said, dismissing them with a wave of his hand.[16]

At some point, however, for the situation to change the rebels have to be seen as people, not thugs. They need to be seen as humans, some of whom earnestly but perhaps misguidedly pursued a path that they felt would lead to a better life. When I talked with Major Carlos Sol, the Philippine army officer put in charge of the Coordinating Committee for the Cessation of Hostilities, he admitted that at first it was difficult for him as an army officer to speak to rebel leaders as equals.[17] But since he was himself from Mindanao and literally spoke the same language as the rebels, he said, he could understand their concerns. Moreover, he said, he was transformed by getting to know the commander of the Moro

Islamic Liberation Force, Butch Malang. As he became acquainted with him, Major Sol said, he was impressed with his integrity and honor. He would have made an excellent officer in the Philippine army, Major Sol suggested. He added that he now regarded Malang not only as a peace partner but as a friend.

One of the jihadi prisoners with whom I spoke in Kurdistan said that all that he and others in the movement wanted was to be treated with dignity. He said that this was the motivation for most who joined the movement. The military destruction of Mosul that led to the end of the territorial control of ISIS simply compounded the situation, he said. Instead of resolving matters, it made them feel all the more humiliated.

In the Punjab, an old Khalistan activist, Gurtej Singh, said much the same thing. As he put it, "all we wanted was respect."[18] Gurtej Singh had been a confidant of the martyred leader Sant Jarnail Singh Bhindranwale, and insisted that Bhindranwale was never in favor of Khalistan, a politically separate state for Sikhs. All he wanted for the Sikh community, Gurtej Singh said, was the honor that they were due as the majority community in the Punjab linguistic region, the post-1966 Punjab State in India. He said that the Sikh uprising was never a terrorist organization, but a movement for Sikh pride. He added that it was a response to the humiliation they felt when Sikhs—particularly those in the dominant rural community, the Jats—were treated as second-class citizens in their own territory, robbed of their water rights and mistreated by the police.

Whether or not Gurtej Singh's analysis was correct, in the period since the cessation of hostilities in the Punjab the Indian government has tried to more visibly show respect to the Sikh community, and to give them greater cultural recognition. Sikh shrines have been improved and recently an enormous government grant provided for a new freeway access and multilevel parking structure adjacent to the Golden Temple. As I mentioned earlier in this book, an elegant marble plaza with fountains and statuary was constructed in the approach to the Sikhs' most sacred shrine. In towns across the Punjab statues have been erected in memorial of historical Sikh figures, such as Bhagat Singh, who was an early nationalist leader in the struggle against the British. Some of the more recent martyrs—the young men killed in the Khalistan uprising—have been memorialized with tacit governmental approval in such villages as Sultanwind, where one of the most prominent young men in the village became the leader of the Khalistan Commando Force, and swallowed a cyanide tablet to kill himself when he was captured by the police. Today, a school library in Sultanwind has been named in his honor.

In Mindanao in the Philippines, travelers entering the urban center of Cotabato City are greeted with a large archway as they arrive at the edge of town from the airport; it is inscribed, "Welcome to the Autonomous Region of Muslim Mindanao." The archway was constructed after the earlier negotiations to create a Muslim Mindanao, but it has been renamed to refer to Bangsamoro, the new political entity created when the plan was finally enacted in 2019. Government agencies in Mindanao that oversee the decommissioning of arms and coordinating the peace process are represented equally by Moro movement leaders and government officials. Each has learned to respect the other. The government also supports local mosques.

On the campus of Notre Dame University in Cotabato City, which was my host for my visits to the region, I found that the university found other ways to use religion in the healing process. A peace research center was established, and the university helped to create an interfaith council in the community. The curriculum itself was a means of reconciliation. Mindanao is a mixed Christian-Muslim population, and the student body in the university is 65 percent Muslim and 35 percent Christian. Since it is a Catholic institution, the Christian students are required to take Bible and Christian theology courses; and the Muslim students are required to take courses in the Qur'an and Muslim theology. Then all students, regardless of religious background, are required to take courses in peace studies and interfaith dialogue to make sure they understand each other's culture.

In Iraq and Syria, it remains to be seen how Sunni Arab culture and leadership will be revered in a post-ISIS society. Though Iraq government support for reconstruction has been slow in coming, investment in former ISIS regions has come from Arab countries such as UAE and Egypt and from private investors. In Ramadi in 2021, a seventy million dollar mall and a twenty-story luxury hotel were constructed with funds from Arab Iraqis abroad. Yet many of the former supporters of ISIS with whom I talked in refugee camps told me that in Iraq the Shi'a continue to treat Sunni "like dirt." One of the former jihadi militants with whom I spoke in prison said that he did not welcome the violence of al-Qaeda and ISIS but that it was necessary. Since the Shi'a government is violent, he said, they had to respond in kind. In his mind, the respect that he craved was not yet forthcoming from the Shi'a-dominated Iraqi government.

In this case, military liberation was only part of the process of reintegration of the Arab Sunni population into the political life of those countries, and it was an incomplete one at that. Full acceptance into the political process is also required. Failing that, the spirit of war will continue, and the conditions will be ripe for a renewal of militant encounter in the future.

Is Cosmic War Conquered?

The lingering longing for a Caliphate and the renewal of images of cosmic war that I heard expressed by ex-jihadi fighters in a Kurdistan prison does not bode well for the disappearance of their imagined wars. In fact, in all three of the cases that I have examined, the image of war has not been dispelled completely. In some cases, though, it has been neutralized. For some, the war spirit has been dampened by being made to feel a part of a multicultural society in which they no longer are treated as marginal and disrespected. In other cases the idea of war has been shelved as old militants sort out their lives in a post-conflict era. Yet the bellicose images remain.

As I talked with the former supporters of the Islamic State I often wondered whether their war was really over. Clearly for Samir and Ahmad, the two men who had escaped Mosul and who I met in the refugee camp, war was a thing of the past and they would never trust the ISIS organization again. I don't know about Hadiya, the woman married to the American ISIS fighter, or Khalid, the cocky detainee suspected of having ISIS ties. If ISIS was reestablished they might find their personal lives enriched by this connection, and they might join it again.

The image of cosmic war was largely expendable for the mass of Sunni Arabs who accepted ISIS provisionally in their opportunistic efforts to restore Sunni Arab power. After all, their motives were largely socio-political rather than ideological. Yet their abandonment of the idea of war cannot be taken for granted. If there are no efforts at conciliation, at granting the tribal leaders the respect and agency that they think they deserve, they could easily support the revival of ISIS or some other radical anti-government opposition. They are still, in a sense, at war with the state, since they think the state is at war with them; if the state's attitude changes—as it did during an earlier period when the Awakening empowered Sunni leaders to rise up against al-Qaeda in Iraq— cosmic war may finally disappear.

But other former jihadi fighters still cling to the possibility that the cosmic war could be revived. Clearly Muhammad and Rahim, the former jihadi warriors with whom I talked in prison, were still ready to fight. There was one moment in my conversation with Muhammad in a room adjacent to the warden's office in the prison where he was incarcerated that I felt some fear for my life. The two of us had been left alone, along with my translator, since the warden trusted Muhammad to be nonviolent. But as Muhammad began to talk about how he still clung to the ideal of a Caliphate and found all of the activities of the Islamic State to be morally justified, his voice began to rise. I began to be nervous. He was a large and healthy man in his late twenties, and I felt weak and small. When Muhammad explicitly said that if the situation was ripe and the movement revived he would willingly kill heretics, specifically Shi'a, along with Jews and Americans, my nervousness turned to apprehension. While he was talking I was holding a pencil to take notes, and realizing in that moment that it could be used as a weapon, I quietly slipped it into my pocket. Seeing me, Muhammad stopped and smiled, and said, "not you, professor, not you."

So whether or not I was seen as a potential enemy in Muhammad's image of cosmic war, the notion of warfare was still a present reality in his mind. I sensed some of the same longing for the old vision of a struggle for Khalistan when I talked with some of the former militant leaders in the Punjab, though not when I talked with the foot soldiers, who seemed broken and disillusioned with warfare. In Mindanao, the image of cosmic war was still alive among the militant stragglers in the mountains, though old leaders such as Butch Malang and Naguib Sinarimbo had long ago accommodated themselves to civil society. But even among them, I sensed a bit of lingering nostalgia for the struggle. Even though they were not ready to strap on weapons and enter into battle again, there was a feeling that the vision and the goals for which they fought were still relevant. Naguib Sinarimbo told me that he had renewed his faith in recent years, and found in his acceptance of a strong and vital engagement with Islam some of the passion that he had earlier found in being part of the militant movement.

The image of war does not dissipate easily. Nor does it need to do so. As long as these images do not lead to real warfare, we can live with them. As one of my former students, Reza Aslan, has asserted in his book, *How to Win a Cosmic War,* often such imagined conflicts cannot be won, but they can be managed.[19] They can continue on in the form of religious language and legendary myth and apocalyptic visions of grand warfare at the end of days. Some in the inner core of the insurgent movements may nurse even the most extreme images of cosmic war in the privacy of their secret gatherings. Every religious community throughout history has had its peculiar ideologues. Often they form marginal groups that communicate largely among themselves and do not surface to public attention unless they are involved in some kind of bizarre behavior. Members of the Heaven's Gate movement in the United States, for instance, believed that they would be taken up into outer space by

UFOs in the last days of the world, a prophecy that was ignored by most people until they committed mass suicide in an attempt to collectively hasten their salvation. Similarly, it is quite possible that the apocalyptic ideas of cosmic war in the ideologies of ISIS, Abu Sayyaf, and the Khalistan movement could continue to exist in small groups that cherish these ideas but do not have the means or the need to force them on others in a violent way.

It may be this mentality that is holding together the inner cores of ISIS and the most radical Moro movements, even at the present moment when their territorial control has collapsed around them. One indication of this is the unwillingness to surrender, accepting a suicidal stance of resistance even in the face of massive opposition and the certainty of defeat. Some who survived, however, lingered on in remote outposts, or in cells like the incarcerated jihadis whom I met in a Kurdistan prison, nursing the pain of losing power but still clinging to the hope of ultimate triumph in a cosmic war.

In considering whether the inner circle of true believers in apocalyptic ideas can be transformed from a terrorist regime to a benign cult, the key question is whether the image of cosmic war can be contained. Once these images of cosmic war have been applied to real situations of territorial struggle and guerilla warfare, can they ever be put back in a metaphorical box? The histories of extreme movements, such as the cases discussed in this book—the Islamic State in Iraq and Syria, the Moro Movement for Muslim Mindanao in the Philippines, and the Khalistan movement of Sikhs in northern India—are accounts of rise and fall, of eruptions into violence and collapse into quiescence. They show that this kind of retreat is possible. At the same time, some people within all of these movements have been convinced that the battles have to be conducted in real time and space in order to be a legitimate form of the cosmic war in which they believe. They have continued to plot schemes of attack, and occasionally conduct them in sporadic terrorist assaults. Ten thousand guerrilla ISIS fighters remained in Iraq and Syria, and hundreds of attacks were conducted in the name of the Islamic State long after its territorial end. In July 2021, for example, ISIS took credit for a suicide bombing in a crowded market in the Shi'a area of Baghdad, killing twenty-seven. In the Philippines, the ISIS-related Abu Sayyaf movement continued to fight on after the peace agreement, and one of the most brutal acts of the Khalistan movement was its last, the 1995 bomb blast that killed Punjab's Chief Minister, Beant Singh.

Other true believers in a movement's cosmic war, however, are able ultimately to accept the idea that the warfare in real time is over. They may still pay their respects to an image of cosmic warfare, but one that they are content to perceive as existing only on a transcendent level. For them, often, the language and legend of religious belief allows them to revive in their imaginations the alternative reality of that worldview, but one that does not intrude into their daily lives. Such language and imagery is the stuff of many religious traditions and does not ordinarily lead to actual instances of violence. In fact, there is a theoretical argument advanced first by Sigmund Freud in *Culture and Its Discontents* and more recently developed by Rene Girard in *Violence and the Sacred* that such symbolic violence is beneficial to a society, since it provides a symbolic displacement for real violence, and thus conduces to peace.[20]

Freud and Girard may or may not be correct, but the fact remains that cosmic war is part of the legendary culture of many traditions. It enriches people's view of the world by helping them imagine deeper forces at work beneath the patina of ordinary reality. These alternative worldviews can be abided by others as long as they do not intrude into their lives, or break into real acts of violence. For it also remains the case that these images endure as resources to be adopted in understanding real confrontations in the world, and in justifying the violence associated with them. Hence, though cosmic war may end as an active agent in violent instances in the three cases that I have examined in the Punjab, Mindanao, and Iraq, it can live on symbolically, perhaps someday to rise again.

Notes

Preface

1. I use the term "Islamic State" interchangeably with the acronym ISIS ("Islamic State of Iraq and Sham," usually translated "Iraq and Syria"). The State Department of the US government often uses the acronym ISIL ("Islamic State of Iraq and the Levant") instead, since the word that the movement uses for Syria is the term for the broader Arabic region including Lebanon, Jordan, and Israel, as well as Syria, a region the French called "the Levant."

2. Mark Juergensmeyer, *Gandhi's Way: A Handbook of Conflict Resolution* (revised and enlarged edition) (Berkeley: University of California Press, 2005).

3. Mark Juergensmeyer, *Global Rebellion: Religious Challenges to the Secular State* (Berkeley: University of California Press, 2008); Mark Juergensmeyer, *Terror in the Mind of God:The Global Rise of Religious Violence*, 4th ed. (Oakland: University of California Press, 2017), original version published in 2000.

4. Mark Juergensmeyer, *The New Cold War? Religious Nationalism Confronts the Secular State* (Berkeley: University of California Press, 1993); revised and enlarged edition published as *Global Rebellion*.

5. Mark Juergensmeyer, Dinah Griego, and John Soboslai, *God in the Tumult of the Global Square: Religion in Global Civil Society* (Berkeley: University of California Press, 2015).

6. Mark Juergensmeyer, *God at War: A Meditation on Religion and Warfare* (New York: Oxford University Press, 2020).

Chapter 1. The Trajectory of Imagined Wars

1. Mark Juergensmeyer, *God at War: A Meditation on Religion and Warfare* (New York: Oxford University Press, 2020). The German version was published as *Krieg und Religion* (Frankfurt: Herder Verlag, 2019).

2. Carl von Clausewitz, *On War*, trans. Michael Howard and Peter Paret (Princeton, NJ: Princeton University Press, 1984), 87. First published posthumously in German as *Vom Kriege* (1832).

3. Juergensmeyer, *God at War*.

4. Mark Juergensmeyer, *Terror in the Mind of God: The Global Rise of Religious Violence*, 4th ed. (Oakland: University of California Press, 2017).

5. Author's interview with Dr. Abdul Aziz Rantisi, co-founder and political head of the Hamas movement, Khan Yunis, Gaza, March 1, 1998.

Chapter 2. The Apocalyptic War of the Islamic State

1. Throughout this book I will use pseudonyms in identifying ordinary supporters of the movement in order to protect their privacy. In the case of public figures, however, I will use their own names.

2. Author's interview with Abdul Salam Al-Kubaisi, Chief of External Relations, Council of Islamic Clergy of al-Anbar Province, Baghdad, May 6, 2004. Translation assistance by Shirouk al-Abayaji.

3. William McCants, *The ISIS Apocalypse: The History, Strategy, and Doomsday Vision of the Islamic State* (New York: St Martin's Press, 2015). See also Graeme Wood, *The Way of the Strangers: Encounters with the Islamic State* (New York: Random House, 2017).

4. Anne Speckhard and Ahmet S. Yayla, *ISIS Defectors: Inside Stories of the Terrorist Caliphate* (McLean, VA: Advances Press, 2016).

5. This may have been the same prison I visited; she does not identify it. Interview published as Anne Speckhard and Ardian Shajkovci, "Confronting an ISIS Emir: ICSVE's Breaking the ISIS Brand Counter-Narratives Project Videos," *Combating Terrorism Exchanged (CTX Journal)* 8, no. 1 (Spring 2018): https://nps.edu/documents/110773463/120099982/CTX+Vol.+8+No.+1.pdf/efddd190-50ac-f843-e915-053b5e792ad8?t=1589841029050#page=6.

6. An account of the German twins who joined ISIS is in my book *God at War: A Meditation on Religion and Warfare* (New York: Oxford University Press, 2020), chapter 4.

7. The Londoner identified as "Jihadi John" was Muhammad Emwazi. The British rap star previously suspected was Abdel-Majed Abdel Bary.

8. Amarnath Amarasingam, "What Twitter Really Means for Islamic State Supporters," *War on the Rocks*, December 30, 2015, https://warontherocks.com /2015/12/what-twitter-really-means-for-islamic-state-supporters.

9. Twitter comment from @gleamingrazor quoted in Azadeh Moaveni, "The Lingering Dream of an Islamic State?," *New York Times*, January 12, 2018, https://www.nytimes.com/2018/01/12/opinion/sunday/post-isis-muslim -homeland.html.

10. Quoted in Moaveni, "The Lingering Dream."

11. Richard Hall, "I Got Cheated, All of Us Got Cheated," *The Independent*, February 8, 2019, https://www.independent.co.uk/news/world/middle-east /isis-syria-fighter-germany-lucas-glass-islamic-state-assad-islam-a8769911 .html.

12. Quoted in Nazim Baksh and Joana Draghici, "No Regret: Captured ISIS Fighter Wants to Return Home—But Not if He Will be Judged by Canadian Law," Canadian Broadcasting Corporation, September 28, 2019, https://www .cbc.ca/news/canada/canadian-isis-fighters-return-home-1.5297142.

13. Amarnath Amarasingam, quoted in Ben Makuch, "An Interview with Abu Hazaifa, Canadian ISIS Fighter," *Vice*, January 17, 2019, https://www.vice.com /en_us/article/8xy4np/an-interview-with-abu-huzaifa-canadian-isis-fighter.

14. Melissa Etehad, "Extremist Finds a New Path," *Los Angeles Times*, Sunday, January 12, 2020, https://enewspaper.latimes.com/infinity/article_share .aspx?guid=b0dbb8cd-664c-4de8-bf6f-0b73be51c45b.

15. Obi Anyadike, "Can You Really 'Deradicalize' a Terrorist?" *MIT Technology Review*, October 24, 2019. https://www.technologyreview.com/s/614569 /deradicalize-terrorist-boko-haram.

Chapter 3. The Militant Struggle of Mindanao Muslims

1. Author's interview with Commander Butch Malang, Cotabato City, Mindanao, Philippines, May 3, 2018.

2. Author's interview with Malang, May 3, 2018.

3. For a good account of the early stages of the Moro movement see Thomas M. McKenna, *Muslim Rulers and Rebels: Everyday Politics and Armed Separatism in the Southern Philippines* (Berkeley: University of California Press, 1998). See also Ben J. Kadil, *The Moro Wars in the Philippines, 1565 to the Present: The Mindanao War of 2003 and the Moro Islamic Liberation Front* (Lewiston, NY: Edwin Mellen Press, 2017).

4. Rommel Banlaoi, *Al-Harakatul Al-Islamiyyah: Essays on the Abu Sayyaf Group, Terrorism in the Philippines from Al Qaeda to ISIS* (Academia Philippine Institute for Peace, Violence and Terrorism Research, n.d.) See also Jeanne K. Giraldo and Harold A. Trinkunas, *Terrorism Financing and State Responses: A Comparative Perspective* (Stanford, CA: Stanford University Press, 2007), 120.

5. Author's interview with Naguib Sinarimbo, Cotabato City, Mindanao, Philippines, May 2, 2018.

6. Author's interview with Pamela Ann Padila, Director of the Planning and Compliance Unit of the Office of the Presidential Adviser on the Peace Process, Government of the Philippines, Manila, August 24, 2016.

7. Author's interview with Sinarimbo, August 22, 2016.

8. Author's interview with Malang, August 23, 2016.

9. Author's interview with Major Carlos Sol, Cotabato City, Mindanao, Philippines, August 23, 2016.

10. See Bob East, *The Neo Abu Sayyaf: Criminality in the Sulu Archipelago of the Republic of the Philippines* (London: Nielsen UK, 2016).

11. Author's interview with Sinarimbo, May 2, 2018.

12. For interesting essays about the 2017 battle of Marawi see Rommel C. Banlaoi, *The Marawi Siege and its Aftermath* (Cambridge: Cambridge Scholars Publishing, 2019).

13. Author's interview with Prof. Achram Latiph, Director of the Institute of Peace and Development Studies, Mindanao State University, Marawi, in Iligan, Mindanao, May 4, 2018.

14. Author's interview with Prof. Drieza Lininding, Institute of Peace and Development Studies, Mindanao State University, in Marawi, May 4, 2018.

15. Author's interview with Michael Saycon, UNICEF Communications Officer, in Manila, May 4, 2018.

16. Author's Interview with Carlos Sol, August 23, 2016.

17. Author's interview with Malang, August 23, 2016.

18. Author's interview with Sinarimbo, May 2, 2018.

19. Author's interview with Zubair Guiaman, Cotabato City, Mindanao, Philippines, May 3, 2018.

20. Author's interview with Malang, May 3, 2018.

Chapter 4. The Fight for Khalistan in India's Punjab

1. Author's interview with Wassan Singh Zaffarwal, Dhariwal, Punjab, January 19, 2017, with arrangement and translation assistance of Prof Jagrup Singh Sekhon.

2. Jyotika Sood, "How Khalistan Movement Scarred Punjab's Very Soul—Wassan Singh Lives to Tell Horror Tales," *Outlook Magazine,* November 18, 2019, https://www.outlookindia.com/magazine/story/india-news-how-khalistan-movement-scarred-punjabs-very-soul-wassan-singh-lives-to-tell-horror-tales/302336.

3. Cynthia Keppley Mahmood, *Fighting for Faith and Nation: Dialogues with Sikh Militants* (Philadelphia: University of Pennsylvania Press, 1996), 152.

4. Mahmood, *Fighting for Faith and Nation,* 155.

5. Paul Wallace, "Terrorism in Punjab & Closure in a Comparative Context: "It Ain't Over 'Till It's Over," *Punjab Journal of Politics* 22, no. 1 (1998): 15.

6. Wallace, "Terrorism in Punjab," 15.

7. Author's interview with Jagtar Singh, Chandigarh, January 17, 2017.

8. Author's interview with Simranjit Singh Mann, Chandigarh, January 17, 2017.

9. Author's interview with Gurtej Singh, Chandigarh, January 18, 2017.

10. Mark Tully and Satish Jacob, *Amritsar: Mrs. Gandhi's Last Battle* (London: Pan Books, 1985); Kuldip Nayar and Khushwant Singh, *Tragedy of Punjab: Operation Bluestar and After* (New Delhi: Vision Books, 1984). See also Manraj Grewal, *Dreams After Darkness: A Search for the Life Ordinary under the Shadow of 1984* (New Delhi: Rupa & Company, 2004).

11. Citizens for Democracy, *Oppression in Punjab* (Columbus, OH: Sikh Religious and Educational Trust, 1985); Gurdev Grewal, *The Searching Eye: An Insider Looks at the Punjab Ordeal* (New Delhi: Rupa & Company, 2006).

12. Sant Jarnail Singh Bhindranwale, "Address to the Sikh Congregation," transcript of a sermon given in the precincts of the Golden Temple, Amritsar,

November 1983, translated by Ranbir Singh Sandhu, distributed by the Sikh Religious and Educational Trust, Dublin, Ohio, April 1985.

13. Bhindranwale, "Address to the Sikh Congregation."

14. Bhindranwale, "Address to the Sikh Congregation."

15. Sant Jarnail Singh Bhindranwale, "Two Lectures" given on July 19 and September 20, 1983, translated by Ranbir Singh Sandhu, distributed by the Sikh Religious and Educational Trust, Dublin, Ohio, 1985.

16. Quoted in Joyce Pettigrew, "In Search of a New Kingdom of Lahore," *Pacific Affairs* 60, no. 1 (Spring 1987): 78–92.

17. Paul Wallace, "Countering Terrorist Movements in India: Kashmir and Khalistan," in *Terrorism and Counterterrorism: Lessons from the Past,* ed. Robert J. Art and Louise Richardson (Washington, DC: United States Institute of Peace Books Press, 2007), 438.

18. Wallace, "Countering Terrorist Movements," 434.

19. Quoted in Ritu Sarin, *The Assassination of Indira Gandhi* (New Delhi: Penguin Books, 1990), 125.

20. Author's interview with Simranjit Singh Mann, Chandigarh, August 3, 1996. For excerpts from my earlier interview with Mann regarding his role in the movement, see *Terror in the Mind of God: The Global Rise of Religious Violence,* 4th ed. (Oakland: University of California Press, 2017), 109ff.

21. Author's interview with Mann, August 3, 1996.

22. Author's interview with Sohan Singh, Mohali, August 4, 1996.

23. Author's interview with Sohan Singh.

24. Mahmood, *Fighting for Faith and Nation.*

25. Mahmood, *Fighting for Faith and Nation,* 149.

26. Author's interview with Sohan Singh.

27. Surjit Singh is a pseudonym chosen to protect the ex-militant's privacy.

28. Author's interview with Surjit Singh, Sultanwind, August 18, 2017.

29. Author's interview with Jagrup Singh Sekhon, Amritsar, August 18, 2017.

30. Harish K. Puri, Paramjit Singh Judge, and Jagrup Singh Sekhon, *Terrorism in Punjab: Understanding Grassroots Reality* (New Delhi: Har-Anand Publications, 1999).

31. Puri, Judge, and Sekhon, *Terrorism in Punjab,* 68–69.

32. Puri, Judge, and Sekhon, *Terrorism in Punjab,* 81.

33. Puri, Judge, and Sekhon, *Terrorism in Punjab,* 84.

34. Thomas Hegghammer, ed., *Jihadi Culture: The Art and Social Practices of Militant Islamists* (Cambridge: Cambridge University Press, 2017).

35. Author's interview with Kanwar Pal Singh Gill, Vrindaban, January 20, 2017.

36. Author's interview with Narinder Singh, Chandigarh, August 4, 1996.

37. Author's interview with Gill.

38. Author's interview with Gill.

39. Author's interview with Narinder Singh.

40. Author's interview with Narinder Singh.

41. Wallace, "Terrorism in Punjab," 15.

42. Wallace, "Terrorism in Punjab," 15.

43. "Virsa Singh Valhora, Ex-Akalie MLA, Acquitted in Murder Case," *The Tribune* (Chandigarh, Punjab), posted June 23, 2021, https://www.tribuneindia.com/news/amritsar/virsa-singh-valtoha-akali-ex-mla-acquitted-in-murder-case-239592. The murder of which Valhora was accused was a 1983 shooting of a Hindu doctor in his clinic in Tarn Taran, Punjab.

44. David Martin and Deepti Hajela, "Protestors Supporting Indian Farmers Demonstrate in NYC," Associate Press, January 26, 2021. https://apnews.com/article/new-york-constitutions-india-narendra-modi-manhattan-b1038d153a556a293c9c407c41b49449.

45. Author's interview with Zaffarwal.

Chapter 5. How Imagined Wars End

1. Author's interview with Wassan Singh Zaffarwal, Dhariwal, January 19, 2017.

2. Author's interview with Naguib Sinarimbo, Cotabato City, Mindanao, Philippines, May 2, 2018.

3. Audrey Kurth Cronin, *How Terrorism Ends: Understanding the Decline and Demise of Terrorist Campaigns* (Princeton, NJ: Princeton University Press, 2011).

4. Isak Svensson, *Ending Holy Wars: Religion and Conflict Resolution in Civil Wars* (Brisbane: University of Queensland Press, 2013).

5. Harish K. Puri, Paramjit Singh Judge, and Jagrup Singh Sekhon, *Terrorism in Punjab: Understanding Grassroots Reality* (Delhi: Har-Anand Publications, 1999).

6. According to figures supplied by the Home Ministry of the Government of India, initially the number of Sikhs killed by Sikh militants in the early 1980s was in the dozens. By 1988 it had swelled to over a thousand. Data reported in the *Times of India*, February 8, 1992, p. 15.

7. Quoted in Shekhar Gupta, "Temple Intrigue," *India Today*, May 15, 1984, 56.

8. Quoted in Gupta, "Temple Intrigue," 57.

9. Ebrahim Moosa, "Overlapping Political Theologies: ISIS and Versions of Sunni Orthodoxy," paper presented at the working group of the project on "Resolving Jihadist Conflicts," Uppsala, Sweden, September 7, 2016.

10. Author's interview with Naguib Sinarimbo, Cotabato City, Mindanao, Philippines, May 2, 2018.

11. Author's interview with Butch Malang, Cotabato City, August 24, 2016.

12. Quoted in Paul Wallace, "Countering Terrorist Movements in India: Kashmir and Khalistan," in *Terrorism and Counterterrorism: Lessons from the Past*, ed. Robert J. Art and Louise Richardson (Washington DC: United States Institute of Peace Books Press, 2007), 432.

13. Wallace, "Countering Terrorist Movements," 436.

14. An article in the *Times of India* in 1988 entitled "Army Wins Hearts in Punjab" describes its role in providing schools, teachers, bridges, footpaths, bus service, agricultural services, sanitation systems, and even sports equipment and coaches. Cited in Wallace, "Countering Terrorist Movements," 434. For the transformation of rebel groups to political parties, see Mimmi Soderberg Kovacs, and Sophi Hatz. "Rebel-to-Party Transformations in Civil War Peace Processes," in *Bullets to Ballots: The Transformation of Rebel Groups into Political Parties*, ed. John Ishiyama (London: Routledge, 2018).

15. Author's interview with Sinarimbo, May 2, 2018.

16. Author's interview with K. P. S. Gill, Vrindaban, January 20, 2017.

17. Author's interview with Major Carlos Sol, Cotabato City, August 24, 2016.

18. Author's interview with Gurtej Singh, Chandigarh, January 17, 2017.

19. Reza Aslan, *How to Win a Cosmic War: God, Globalization, and the End of the War on Terror* (New York: Random House, 2009).

20. Sigmund Freud, *Civilization and Its Discontents*, trans. James Strachey (New York: Norton, 1961 [1929]); Rene Girard, *Violence and the Sacred*, trans. Patrick Gregory (Baltimore: Johns Hopkins University Press, 1977 [1972]).

Interviews

Adjerol-Morados, Dean Macrina. Shari'ah Counsellor, Institute of Islamic Studies, University of the Philippines. Dilman Campus, Manila, August 22, 2016.

Ahmad (pseudyonym, no last name given). Hasan Sham Refugee Camp, Kurdistan, Iraq. March 10, 2019.

Ahmed, Musa. Head, Barzani Charitable Foundation. Erbil, March 10, 2019.

Algabre, Sheila. Vice President for Administration, Notre Dame University. Erbil, August 24, 2016; May 1, 2018; and August 23, 2019.

Al-Kubaisi, Abdul Salam. Chief of External Relations, Council of Islamic Clergy of Al-Anbar Province. Baghdad, May 6, 2004. Translation assistance by Shirouk al-Abayaji.

Al-Talabani, Major-General Jalal Naji. Chief, Peshmerga Intelligence Agency, Force 70. Suliamani, March 13, 2019.

Arslan, Cihangir. President, Pacific Dialogue Foundation. Manila, August 22, 2016.

Cura, Dean Fatih. Dean of Management School, Tishk University. Erbil, March 11, 2019.

De Guzman, Judith. Officer in Charge, Monetary Foundation, Data Management, Office of the Presidential Advisory for the Peace Process. Manila, August 18, 2016.

Gill, Kanwar Pal Singh. Former Head of Punjab Police. Vrindaban, January 20, 2017.

Guiaman, Zubair. Volunteer, Moro Islamic Liberation Front Youth Outreach Program. Cotabato City, May 3, 2018.

Hadiya (pseudyonym, no last name given). Hasan Sham Refugee Camp, Kurdistan, Iraq. February 12, 2017.

Hamad, Prof. Dilshad. Head, International Relations and Diplomacy Department, Tishk University. Erbil, March 10, 2019.

Inzon, Fr. Charlie M., OMI. President, Notre Dame University. Erbil, August 23, 2016.

Irwani, Muslih. Founding Director, Public Policy Institute. Erbil, March 11, 2019.

Kadil, Prof. Alono. Notre Dame University. Erbil, August 23, 2016.

Khalid (pseudyonym, no last name given). Hasan Sham Refugee Camp, Kurdistan, Iraq. March 10, 2019.

Latiph, Prof. Achram. Director of the Institute of Peace and Development Studies, Mindanao State University, Marawi. Iligan, Mindanao, May 4, 2018.

Lingga, Prof. Abou. Member, Peace Implementation Panel, Moro Islamic Liberation Front. Cotabato City, May 2, 2018.

Lininding, Prof. Drieza. Institute of Peace and Development Studies, Mindanao State University. Marawi, May 4, 2018.

Malang, Commander Butch. Co-Director, Coordinating Committee for the Cessation of Hostilities. Cotabato City, Mindanao, August 24, 2016 and May 3, 2018.

Mann, Simranjit Singh. Chandigarh, August 3, 1996 and January 17, 2017.

Muhammad (pseudonym; no last name given). Kurdistan prison, March 13, 2019.

Omar (pseudyonym, no last name given). Hasan Sham Refugee Camp, Kurdistan, Iraq, February 12, 2017.

Padila, Pamela Ann. Director of the Planning and Compliance Unit of the Office of the Presidential Adviser on the Peace Process, Government of the Philippines. Manila, August 24, 2016.

Rahim (pseudonym; no last name given). Kurdistan prison, March 13, 2019.

Rantisi, Abdul Aziz. Co-founder and political head of the Hamas movement. Khan Yunis, Gaza, March 1, 1998.

Salih, Idris Hali. President and Head of Board of Trustees, Tishk University. Erbil, March 11, 2019.

Samir (pseudonym, no last name given). Hasan Sham Refugee Camp, Kurdistan, Iraq, March 12, 2019.

Saycon, Michael. Communications Officer, United Nations Children's Fund (UNICEF). Manila, May 4, 2018.

Sekhon, Prof Jagrup Singh. Chair, Department of Political Science, Guru Nanak Dev University. Amritsar, August 18, 2017.

Sinarimbo, Naguib. Minister of the Interior and Local Government, Bangsamoro Autonomous Region in Muslim Mindanao. Cotabato City, Mindanao, August 22, 2016, May 1, 2018, and May 2, 2018.

Singh, Gurtej. Chandigarh, January 17 and January 18, 2017.

Singh, Jagtar. Chandigarh, January 17, 2017.

Singh, Narinder. Chandigarh, August 4, 1996.

Singh, Sohan. Mohali, August 4, 1996.

Singh, Surjit (pseudonym). Sultanwind, August 18, 2017.

Sinjari, Karim. Minister of Interior, Kurdistan Regional Government. Erbil, March 11, 2019.

Sol, Major Carlos. Co-Director of the Coordinating Committee for the Cessation of Hostilities. Cotabato City, Mindanao, August 23 and August 24, 2016.

Tanada, Karen N. Director, Gaston Z. Ortigas Peace Institute, Ateneo de Manila University. Manila, August 22, 2016.

Zabala, Fr. Francis, OMI. President, Notre Dame University. Cotabato City, May 1, 2018.

Zaffarwal, Wassan Singh. Dhariwal, Punjab. January 19, 2017.

Bibliography

Amarsingam, Amarnath. "What Twitter Really Means for Islamic State Supporters," *War on the Rocks*, December 30, 2015. https://warontherocks .com/2015/12/what-twitter-really-means-for-islamic-state-supporters.

Anyadike, Obi. "Can You Really 'Deradicalize' a Terrorist?" *MIT Technology Review*, October 24, 2019. https://www.technologyreview.com/s/614569 /deradicalize-terrorist-boko-haram.

Aslan, Reza. *How to Win a Cosmic War: God, Globalization, and the End of the War on Terror*. New York: Random House, 2009.

Baksh, Nazim, and Joana Draghici. "No Regret: Captured ISIS Fighter Wants to Return Home—But Not if He Will be Judged by Canadian Law." Canadian Broadcasting Corporation, September 28, 2019. https://www .cbc.ca/news/canada/canadian-isis-fighters-return-home-1.5297142.

Banlaoi, Rommel. *Al-Harakatul Al-Islamiyyah: Essays on the Abu Sayyaf Group, Terrorism in the Philippines from Al Qaeda to ISIS*. Academia Philippine Institute for Peace, Violence and Terrorism Research, n.d.

Banlaoi, Rommel C. *The Marawi Siege and its Aftermath*. Cambridge: Cambridge Scholars Publishing, 2019.

Bhindranwale, Sant Jarnail Singh. "Address to the Sikh Congregation," transcript of a sermon given in the precincts of the Golden Temple, Amritsar, November 1983, translated by Ranbir Singh Sandhu. Dublin, OH: Sikh Religious and Educational Trust, April 1985.

———. "Two Lectures," given on July 19 and September 20, 1983, translated by Ranbir Singh Sandhu. Dublin, OH: Sikh Religious and Educational Trust, 1985.

Citizens for Democracy. *Oppression in Punjab.* Columbus, OH: Sikh Religious and Educational Trust, 1985.

Cronin, Audrey Kurth. *How Terrorism Ends: Understanding the Decline and Demise of Terrorist Campaigns.* Princeton, NJ: Princeton University Press, 2011.

East, Bob. *The Neo Abu Sayyaf: Criminality in the Sulu Archipelago of the Republic of the Philippines.* London: Nielsen UK, 2016.

Etehad, Melissa. "Extremist Finds a New Path." *Los Angeles Times,* January 12, 2020. https://enewspaper.latimes.com/infinity/article_share.aspx?guid= b0dbb8cd-664c-4de8-bf6f-0b73be51c45b.

Freud, Sigmund. *Civilization and Its Discontents,* translated by James Strachey. New York: Norton, 1961 [1929].

Giraldo, Jeanne K., and Harold A. Trinkunas. *Terrorism Financing and State Responses: A Comparative Perspective.* Stanford, CA: Stanford University Press, 2007.

Gupta, Shekhar. "Temple Intrigue." *India Today,* May 15, 1984.

Girard, Rene. *Violence and the Sacred,* translated by Patrick Gregory. Baltimore: Johns Hopkins University Press, 1977 [1972].

Grewal, Manraj. *Dreams After Darkness: A Search for the Life Ordinary Under the Shadow of 1984.* New Delhi: Rupa & Company, 2004.

Grewal, Gurdev. *The Searching Eye: An Insider Looks at the Punjab Ordeal.* New Delhi: Rupa & Co, 2006.

Hall, Richard. "I Got Cheated, All of Us Got Cheated." The Independent, February 8, 2019. https://www.independent.co.uk/news/world/middle-east/isis-syria-fighter-germany-lucas-glass-islamic-state-assad-islam-a8769911.html.

Hegghammer, Thomas. *Jihadi Culture: The Art and Social Practices of Militant Islamists.* Cambridge: Cambridge University Press, 2017.

Juergensmeyer, Mark. *Gandhi's Way, A Handbook of Conflict Resolution.* Revised and enlarged edition. Berkeley: University of California Press, 2005.

———. *Global Rebellion: Religious Challenges to the Secular State.* Berkeley: University of California Press, 2008. Revised version of *The New Cold War? Religious Nationalism Confronts the Secular State,* 1993.

———. *Terror in the Mind of God: The Global Rise of Religious Violence.* 4th ed. Oakland: University of California Pres, 2018.

——— *God at War: A Meditation on Religion and Warfare*. New York: Oxford University Press, 2020.

———, Dinah Griego, and John Soboslai. *God in the Tumult of the Global Square: Religion in Global Civil Society*. Berkeley: University of California Press, 2015.

Kadil, Ben J. *The Moro Wars in the Philippines, 1565 to the Present: The Mindanao War of 2003 and the Moro Islamic Liberation Front*. Lewiston NY: Edwin Mellen Press, 2017.

Kovacs, Mimmi Soderberg, and Sophi Hatz. "Rebel-to-Party Transformations in Civil War Peace Processes." In *Bullets to Ballots: The Transformation of Rebel Groups into Political Parties*, edited by John Ishiyama. London: Routledge, 2018.

Makuch, Ben. "An Interview with Abu Hazaifa, Canadian ISIS Fighter." *Vice*, January 17, 2019. https://www.vice.com/en_us/article/8xy4np/an-interview-with-abu-huzaifa-canadian-isis-fighter.

Mahmood, Cynthia Keppley. *Fighting for Faith and Nation: Dialogues with Sikh Militants*. Philadelphia: University of Pennsylvania Press, 1996.

McCants, William. *The ISIS Apocalypse: The History, Strategy, and Doomsday Vision of the Islamic State*. New York: St Martin's Press, 2015.

McKenna, Thomas M. *Muslim Rulers and Rebels: Everyday Politics and Armed Separatism in the Southern Philippines*. Berkeley: University of California Press, 1998.

Moaveni, Azadeh. "The Lingering Dream of an Islamic State?" *New York Times*, January 12, 2018, https://www.nytimes.com/2018/01/12/opinion/sunday/post-isis-muslim-homeland.html.

Mussa, Ebrahim. "Overlapping Political Theologies: ISIS and Versions of Sunni Orthodoxy." Paper presented at the working group of the project on "Resolving Jihadist Conflicts," Uppsala, Sweden, September 7, 2016.

Nayar, Kuldip, and Khushwant Singh. *Tragedy of Punjab: Operation Bluestar and After*. New Delhi: Vision Books, 1984.

Pettigrew, Joyce. "In Search of a New Kingdom of Lahore." *Pacific Affairs* 60, no. 1 (Spring 1987): 78–92.

Puri, Harish K., Paramjit Singh Judge, and Jagrup Singh Sekhon. *Terrorism in Punjab: Understanding Grassroots Reality*. New Delhi: Har-Anand Publications, 1999.

Sarin, Ritu. *The Assassination of Indira Gandhi*. New Delhi: Penguin Books, 1990.

Sood, Jyotika. "How Khalistan Movement Scarred Punjab's Very Soul— Wassan Singh Lives to Tell Horror Tales." *Outlook Magazine,* November 18, 2019. https://www.outlookindia.com/magazine/story/india-news -how-khalistan-movement-scarred-punjabs-very-soul-wassan-singh -lives-to-tell-horror-tales/302336.

Speckhard, Anne, and Ardian Shajkovci. "Confronting an ISIS Emir: ICSVE's Breaking the ISIS Brand Counter-Narratives Project Videos." *Combating Terrorism Exchanged (CTX Journal)* 8, no. 1 (Spring 2018). https://nps.edu /documents/110773463/120099982/CTX+Vol.+8+No.+1.pdf/efddd190 -50ac-f843-e915-053b5e792ad8?t=1589841029050#page=6.

Speckhard, Anne, and Ahmet S. Yayla. *ISIS Defectors: Inside Stories of the Terrorist Caliphate*. McLean, VA: Advances Press, 2016.

Svensson, Isak. *Ending Holy Wars: Religion and Conflict Resolution in Civil Wars*. Brisbane: University of Queensland Press, 2013.

Tully, Mark, and Satish Jacob. *Amritsar: Mrs. Gandhi's Last Battle.* London: Pan Books, 1985.

von Clausewitz, Carl. *On War*, translated by Michael Howard and Peter Paret. Princeton, NJ: Princeton University Press, 1984 [1832].

Wallace, Paul. "Countering Terrorist Movements in India: Kashmir and Khalistan," in *Terrorism and Counterterrorism: Lessons from the Past,* edited by Robert J. Art and Louise Richardson, 425–82. Washington, DC: United States Institute of Peace Books Press, 2007.

———. "Terrorism in Punjab & Closure in a Comparative Context: It 'Ain't' Over 'Till It's Over." *Punjab Journal of Politics* 22, no. 1 (1998): 4–24.

Wood, Graeme. *The Way of the Strangers: Encounters with the Islamic State.* New York: Random House, 2017.

Index

absolute war, 5–9; change of attitude towards, 3–4; cosmic war and, 12; defining, 5–6, 8; religion and, 9, 12. *See also* imagined wars

Abu Sayyaf (Moro extremist faction): apocalyptic ideology of, 146, 147; ending of, 126; formation of, 59–60; founder of, 59, 67; Hapilon and, 67, 73–74, 79; ISIS and, 67; Marawi siege (2017), 70, 71–74, 82; military actions against, 136; peace negotiations and, 56, 129; support of, 67–68; violence of, 63, 66–67. *See also* Janjalani, Abdurajik Abubakar

"Address to the Sikh Congregation" (sermon transcript) (Bhindranwale), 153n12

Adjerol-Morados, Dean Macrina, 157

Afghanistan: Gill doctrine and, 111; Janjalani in, 59; Taliban movement, 125

Ahmad (interviewee): about, 18–19, 157; view of ISIS, 19–20, 20–21, 23, 31, 143

Ahmed, Musa, 157

Akal Federation, 113

Akali-BJP coalitions, 100

Akali Dal, 96, 100, 113

Algabre, Sheila, 157

All-India Sikh Students Federation, 98

alternative realities: competing, 10; cosmic war as fusion of, 11–14; imagined wars as, 9; religion as, 9–10

Amarasingam, Amarnath, 49, 52

al-Anbar province, 27, 150n2, 157

apocalyptic ideology: of Abu Sayyaf (Moro extremist faction), 146, 147; as fundamental to ISIS leaders, 11; of ISIS caliphate, 32–33, 42, 126; of Islamic State, 37–38, 40–46; of Khalistan movement, 146–47; Mahdi (Islamic savior), 41–42, 42; Marawi apocalypse, 126; of Moro movement, 146–47. *See also* Islamic State (ISIS), apocalyptic war of

Aquino, Benigno, 81
Aquino, Corazon, 58
Arab Spring, 35, 135
ARMM (Autonomous Region of Muslim Mindanao), 58, 60, 62–63, 64, 81
"Army Wins Hearts in Punjab," 156n14
Aslan, Reza, 145
al-Assad, Bashar, 29
authorities: civil acceptance and, 136–38; conveying of hope by, 139; extrajudicial killings and, 134; military assaults and, 134–35; rebel movements and, 130–31; strong limitations and, 130–36. *See also specific governments*
Autonomous Region of Muslim Mindanao (ARMM), 58, 60, 62–63, 64, 81
Awakening movement, 35, 144

Babbar Khalsa, 89, 92, 98, 123
al-Baghdadi, Abu Bakr: as Caliph, 36, 42, 125; credentials of, 43–44; death of, 50, 126; Filipino militants and, 67, 72; global jihadi movement and, 48; Islamic State and, 28–30; recruitment strategy of, 46
al-Baghdadi, Abu Omar, 28
Bangsamoro Autonomous Region of Muslim Mindanao, 60, 63–64, 81, 84–85, 141
Bangsamoro Islamic Armed Forces, 56
Bangsamoro Islamic Freedom Fighters (BIFF), 56, 66, 68, 81–82, 124, 128, 129

Bangsamoro Liberation Organization, 57
Bangsamoro peace agreement (2014): in 1996, 60; in 2014, 65, 66, 81; in 2018, 1, 84–85; Abu Sayyaf movement after, 147; Duterte and, 64–65, 84; as unratified, 69, 83
Bary, Abdel Majed Abdel, 151n7
battles: epic Indian battle stories, 11; for Khalistan, 94–104, 110–15; for Mosul, 2; participant attitudes about, 3; spiritual battle template, 12–13. *See also* Marawi siege (2017)
beheadings, 27, 28, 30, 45–46, 47, 51, 67
Bhartiya Janata Party (Indian People's Party) (BJP), 100
Bhindranwale, Jarnail Singh: Dal Khalsa and, 96; death of, 88, 103, 124, 126; Gurtej Singh and, 140; Khalistan and, 94; Khalistan movement and, 95–96; sermons of, 97–98, 153n12; Surjit Singh and, 105; turban preference of, 87; Zaffarwal and, 88
Bhindranwale Tiger Force, 89, 97, 98, 123
Bible, 11, 142
BJP (Bhartiya Janata Party) (Indian People's Party), 100
Boko Haram, 53
bombings: Brussels bombings (2016), 48; Davao City bombing (2016), 68; suicide bombings, 12, 47, 47–48, 128; suicides, 44, 147; Superferry 14 bombing (2004), 59–60
Bosnian conflict, 61

hope: alternative opportunities and, 120; apocalyptic ideology and, 146; Bangsamoro peace agreement (2014) and, 64, 83; Caliphate and, 50; conveying of, 138–43; deferred, 44; end of movements and, 3, 24, 127–29; for ISIS outpost in Philippines, 72

houris, 13

How Terrorism Ends (Cronin), 118

How to Win a Cosmic War (Aslan), 145

ideal war, 8, 81. *See also* absolute war

imagined wars: about, 1–5; absolute war and, 5–9; as alternative reality, 9; cosmic war as alternative realities fusion, 11–14; defining, 5, 6–7; non-war, war, and cosmic war, 14–17; religion and war, 9–11

imagined wars, end of: about, 116–19; cosmic war as conquered, 143–48; Cronin on, 118; external conditions, 117, 130–43; internal conditions, 117, 119–30; non-war as, 15; participant attitudes about, 3; Svensson on, 118. *See also* external conditions of imagined wars end; internal conditions of imaged wars end

India: epic battle stories in popular media, 11; Indian farmers protest movement, 115

Indian Airlines hijacking, 96

Indian government: agricultural legislation of, 115; as identified enemy, 7; Khalistan movement and, 99–100, 130, 132–33; Mann on decline of, 101; Sikh support by, 114, 140–41

Indonesia, 56, 59, 74

internal conditions of imaged wars end: about, 119–20; communal consensus fractures, 123–27; hope, 127–29; loss of faith, 120–23

International Islamic Relief Organization, 59

Inzon, Charlie M, 158

Iraq: anarchy in western, 135; Iraqi army and ISIS, 131; ISIS' territorial claims in, 26; post-ISIS society in, 142; post-Saddam, 2, 20; pro-Shi'a bias in, 2, 20, 25, 138; Sunni leaders in, 137; US-led invasion of, 18, 26–27, 135; U.S. occupation of, 138; al-Zarqawi, Abu Musab, 27–28, 35, 42, 44. *See also* Mosul

Iraqi government: former ISIS fighters and, 138; ISIS and, 30, 130, 138; Shi'a control and, 20, 25, 142

Irwani, Muslim, 158

ISIL (Islamic State of Iraq and the Levant), 2, 26, 149n1

ISIS (Islamic State of Iraq and Sham). *See* Islamic State of Iraq and Sham (ISIS)

ISIS-branded movements: Maute group, 68–69, 73; in Mindanao, 68–69, 82. *See also* Abu Sayyaf (Moro extremist faction); Bangsamoro Islamic Freedom Fighters (BIFF); Moro Islamic Liberation Front (MILF)

Islam: converts to, 51; imams, 21, 38, 43, 52, 129; ISIS ideology and, 43; Islamic State and, 40; Wahhabi Islam, 27, 42, 45–46, 59

comparisons to, 94, 95, 100; end of, 110–15, 120, 132–33; Hindu nationalism and, 100; identifying enemy of, 7; Indian government, 99–100, 100; infighting and schisms, 123–24; leadership of, 113, 120, 128, 137, 141; participant attitudes about, 3, 139; police and, 108, 111–12, 114, 115, 119, 130, 132–33, 134, 136, 139; political goals, 99, 137; renewed interest in, 114–15; Surjit Singh and, 104–9; violence of, 147; worldview of, 16, 107–9, 117–18; Zaffarwal and, 87–94. *See also* Gill, Kanwar Pal Singh; Sikh militants; Sikh moderates; Singh, Surjit

kidnappings: Abu Sayyaf and, 60, 63, 66–67; in Marawi, 75–76; by militant Sikhs, 99; Samal Island kidnappings (2016), 66–67

Kitab at-Tawhid (*The Book of Divine Unity*) (al-Wahhabi), 45

Krieg und Religion (Juergensmeyer), 150n1(ch1)

Al-Kubaisi, Abdul Salam, 150n2(ch2)

Kurdish Peshmerga, 136

Kurdistan region: prisoners in, 31, 45, 54, 140, 143, 146, 158; radio broadcasts from, 20; refugee camps in, 17, 157, 158; refugees in, 23, 24, 31, 157, 158

bin Laden, Osama, 27–28, 33, 37, 44, 59, 125

Latiph, Achram, 158

leaders: adaptation of, 128–29, 137; authority of, 125–26; death of,

125–26; end of movements and, 118, 119–20, 125–26, 137; Sunni tribal leaders, 35, 137; Taliban movement, 125; uncompromising attitude of, 12. *See also specific leaders*

Lebanon, 26, 149n1

Levant, 26, 149n1

Libya, 47, 58, 59

limitations, effects of, 130–36

Lingga, Abou, 158

Lininding, Drieza, 158

Madani, Iyad Ameen, 43

Magsaysay, Ramon, 57

Maguindanao, 62, 68

Mahabharata (Vyasa), 11

Mahdi (Islamic savior), 41–42, 42

Mahmood, Cynthia Keppley, 103

Malang, Butch: adaptation of, 145; Bangsamoro peace agreement (2014), 85; on extremists, 65–66, 69; interview, 158; as MILF commander, 55–56; peace negotiations, 80–83, 84, 129; Sol and, 140; on splinter groups, 124

Malaysia, 56, 74

al-Maliki, Nouri, 29

Mamasapano incident, 64, 65

Mann, Simranjit Singh, 94, 100–102, 104, 111, 120, 137, 158

Manochahal, Gurbachan Singh, 89

Marawi siege (2017): aftermath of, 75–80, 83–84, 126; events of, 69–74; military confrontation, 1; peace process and, 82; resentments after, 77–79, 83, 84, 134; UNICEF and, 80. *See also* Maute group

Marcos, Ferdinand, 57

marginalization: global jihadi movement and, 49, 50; neutralization of, 143; in post-ISIS period, 137; Punjab government policies and, 95; religious communities and, 145; of Sunni Arabs, 7, 27, 29

martyrdom: in Christianity, 13; Hamas movement and, 126; inspiration of, 126; in Islam, 13; Sikh community and, 91, 96, 140, 141; suicide missions as, 44, 47. *See also* suicides

al-Masri, Abu Ayyub, 28, 42

Maute, Abdullah Jakul, 68, 73, 74, 82

Maute, Jorge Salsalani, 68

Maute, Omar, 68, 73, 74, 82

Maute, Ominta Romato, 68, 73

Maute group, 68, 70, 71–74, 73, 79, 82, 126

McCants, William, 42

MILF (Moro Islamic Liberation Front). *See* Moro Islamic Liberation Front (MILF)

military forces: Bangsamoro Islamic Freedom Fighters (BIFF), 56, 66; imagined wars' end and, 131–36, 137; peace process and, 1–2. *See also* Marawi siege (2017)

Mindanao, Philippines: about, 55–56; Davao City bombing (2016), 68; diversification of, 57; lack of village-level authority, 135; Maguindanao language, 62; Maguindanao region, 68; Moro movement leaders in, 141; Muslim movements in, 57, 68; Samal Island kidnappings, 66–67; during WWII, 57. *See also* Marawi; Sulu peninsula

Mindanao Muslims: identified enemy of, 7; as Moros, 56; origins of, 56; self-rule, 81. *See also* Moros

Mindanao State University, 61, 69, 71

miri-piri concept, 97–98

MNLF (Moro National Liberation Front). *See* Moro National Liberation Front (MNLF)

Moosa, Ebrahim, 125

morality: moral authority of Sikh militants, 103–4; religious aspects of, 8, 9; of war, 5–6

Moro Islamic Liberation Front (MILF): Abu Sayyaf and, 66; ARMM and, 58; Bangsamoro Islamic Armed Forces, 56; Bangsamoro peace agreement (2014) and, 85; BIFF and, 124; comparisons to, 94; cosmic war ideology of, 135; ISIS rebels and, 82–83; leadership of, 55–56, 62, 63, 65, 81–82, 139–40; Mamasapano incident, 64, 65; negotiations with, 1–2, 55–56, 63, 124; religion and, 129; Salamat and, 63; violence of extremists, 65–69; Youth Outreach Program, 84. *See also* Malang, Butch; Maute group; Sinarimbo, Naguib

Moro militants: Bangsamoro Islamic Freedom Fighters (BIFF), 56, 66, 68–69; demilitarization of, 65; Maute group, 68–69, 73. *See also* Abu Sayyaf (Moro extremist faction); Moro Islamic Liberation

41–42; Sunni Arabs against, 144; view of, 119, 142. *See also* al-Baghdadi, Abu Bakr; bin Laden, Osama; al-Masri, Abu Ayyub; al-Zarqawi, Abu Musab

qaum (community), 97

Quezon, Manuel, 57

Qur'an, 13, 43, 142

Rabbani, Imran, 52–53

Rahim (interviewee), 38–39, 44, 144, 158

Ramadi, 30, 31, 136, 137, 142

Ramayana, 11

Ramos, Fidel, 59

Rantisi, Abdul Aziz, 12–13, 15, 158. *See also* Hamas movement

rebel movements: authorities response to, 130–31; infighting and schisms, 126; infighting within, 126; leaders of, 125–26; religious factor in, 118; supporters of, 136–37. *See also* Islamic State of Iraq and Sham (ISIS); Khalistan movement; Moro movement

reconciliation: in Iraq, 140, 142–43; in Philippines, 141–42; in Punjab, 140–41

recruitment of ISIS: global jihadi movement and, 46–54; stages of, 40–41

refugee camps: Hasan Sham Refugee Camp (Kurdistan, Iraq), 2, 17, 23, 157, 158; interviews in, 2, 5, 17, 29. *See also specific interviewees*

religion: as alternative reality, 9–10, 147–48; Babbar Khalsa and, 89; as factor in rebel movements, 118; in

healing process, 141–42, 145; idea of war and, 7–8; metaphorical use of war, 10; Moro movement and, 62, 63, 129; in peace process, 129; relations to violence, 4–5, 11, 67; relations to war, 5; religious legitimization, 8, 10; scriptural war references, 11; Sikh militants and, 108; warfare and, 9–11, 14, 145

religious wars: cosmic war concept, 11; worldview shifts, 4. *See also* cosmic war

reorientation to nonviolence, 118

Ridwan, Abu (Muhammad Khalifa), 51

Romania, 99

rule of law: firm limitations and, 135; importance of, 134

Rumiyah (ISIS online magazine), 42

Saddam regime: life after, 2, 5, 6, 20, 33, 38, 138; Sunni Arabs in, 18, 27

Salamat, Hashim, 63

Salih, Idris Hali, 158

salvation, 13, 43, 146

salwar-kameez (Punjabi women's clothing), 89

Samal Island kidnappings (2016), 66–67

Samir (interviewee): about, 18, 158; escape from Mosul, 22–23; view of ISIS, 20, 21, 31, 143

San Bernardino attack (2016), 48

Sant Nirankaris, 95–96

Satan/satanic powers: of enemies, 13–14; enemies as agents of, 13, 15; idea of war and, 8

Saudi Arabia: Janjalani in, 59; MNLF and, 58, 59; rebel fighters from, 74; remittance money from, 76; terrorists from, 48; Wahhabi Islam, 27, 45–46, 59

Saycon, Michael, 159

scriptures: al-Baghdadi and, 43; Hebrew bible, 11, 142; Hindu epics, 11; Qur'an, 13, 43, 142; Sikh scriptures, 108

secularism, Bhindranwale on, 97

secular political orders: as enemy, 8; in India, 98; of Saddam, 27; Sikhs and, 95, 97, 98, 100; in U.S. and Europe, 48

Sekhon, Jagrup Singh, 86, 107–9, 108, 109, 159

Shajkovci, Ardian, 150n5(ch2)

shari'a laws, 43, 45–46

Shi'a Arabs: in Iraq, 30–31; Islamic State and, 37; in liberation troops, 136; al-Qaeda and, 33–34; Sunni Arabs and, 5, 7, 24–25, 27; Sunni Arabs view of, 20, 38, 142–43

Shi'a control: al-Maliki and, 28–29; in post-Saddam Iraq, 2, 20, 27; Sunni Arabs under, 37–38

Shi'a Islam, in Syria, 29

Sikh (term), meaning of, 103

Sikhism: Bhindranwale on community among, 97; community guidance in, 103; national visibility of, 114; Sikh farmers, 115; violence and, 101–2, 103, 104

Sikh militants: Alaki party and, 87–88; Bhindranwale, 88, 94, 95, 96, 105, 124, 135, 140; in hiding, 101, 113; leadership of, 101; Mahmood on, 103; Mann on

decline of, 101; moral authority of, 103–4; radical organizations of, 98; renewed protest by, 114–15; Romanian government and, 99; Sikhs killed by, 156n6; Sohan Singh on, 102–4; study on, 107–9; Surjit Singh on, 104–7; violence in Punjab, 98–99; worldview of, 16, 109. *See also* Bhindranwale, Jarnail Singh; Khalistan movement; Mann, Simranjit Singh

Sikh moderates, 95, 99–100; as identified enemy, 7

Sikhs: 1980s uprising, 95, 104, 109, 140; 1984 massacres of, 97; Akali-BJP coalitions and, 100; Jat Sikhs, 95; in KCF, 90–91; killed by Sikh militants, 156n6; Sant Nirankaris and, 95–96; support of, 140–41

Sikh separatist movement. *See* Khalistan movement

Sikh state. *See* Khalistan

Sikh Students Federation, 89, 124–25

sin, Sikh view of, 98, 109

Sinarimbo, Naguib: about, 60–61; adaptation of, 116, 145; in Bangsamoro government, 85; during Marawi siege (2017), 69–74, 82–83; MILF and, 62–63; Muslim activism of, 61–62; peace negotiations, 63–65, 82–83, 127–28, 138–39

Singh, Baba Deep, 96

Singh, Beant, 100, 102, 103, 104, 111, 147

Singh, Bhagat, 141

Singh, Bhai Dhanna, 103

Singh, Gurtej, 95, 140, 159

Singh, Harjinder "Jinda," 90, 91, 97
Singh, Jagtar, 94, 159
Singh, Jarnail, 95–96
Singh, Labh (Sukhdev "Sukha"
    Singh), 90, 132–33
Singh, Manmohan, 114
Singh, Narinder, 111, 112–13, 120, 159
Singh, Sohan, 102, 103–4, 120, 159
Singh, Sukhdev "Sukha" (Labh
    Singh), 90, 91, 97, 132–33
Singh, Surjit, 104–9, 120, 122, 130,
    154n27, 159
Singh, Zail, 96
Sinjari, Karim, 159
social anomalies, war as response
    to, 6
social discord, use of, 7, 10
social media, global jihadi move-
    ment and, 46–54
Sodhi, Surinder Singh, 124
Sol, Carlos, 66, 80–82, 139, 159
Spain: conquest of Philippines by, 56;
    Spanish-American War, 57;
    Zaffarwal in, 93
splinter groups, 123–25
Sri Lanka, 111
suicides: of leaders, 90, 126; mass
    suicides, 146; suicide bombings,
    12, 44, 47, 47–48, 128, 147. See also
    martyrdom
Sukha (Sukhdev Singh), 90, 91, 97,
    132–33
Sultanwind (village), 104–5, 106,
    109, 141
Sultanwind, Kanwarjit Singh, 90,
    141
Sulu peninsula, 56, 59, 62, 67–68
Sunni Arabs: Awakening movement,
    35; empowerment movements for,

26–31, 35–36; in Fallujah, 137; fears
    in post-Saddam world, 6, 7, 18, 20,
    27; ISIS and, 29–30; Islamic State
    and, 2, 143–44; in liberation
    troops, 136; al-Maliki and, 28–29;
    marginalization of, 7, 20, 29; on
    Mosul, 134; al-Qaeda and, 33; in
    Ramadi, 137; on Raqqa, 134; Shi'a
    Arabs and, 5, 20, 24–25, 142–43;
    under Shi'a control, 37–38;
    al-Zarqawi, 27–28, 35, 42, 44. See
    also Muhammad (interviewee)
Superferry 14 bombing (2004),
    59–60
Svensson, Isak, 118
Switzerland, 93
symbolic violence, 147
Syria: anarchy in eastern, 135;
    al-Baghdadi in, 36; ISIL (term)
    usage and, 149n1; ISIS' territorial
    claims in, 26; Janjalani in, 59;
    al-Kanadi in, 52; Khalifa in, 51;
    post-ISIS society in, 142; Sunni
    leaders in, 137; Sunni uprising in,
    29; Syrian army and ISIS, 131

al-Talabani, Jalal Naji., 157
Taliban movement, 125
Tanada, Karen N., 159
terrorism: militarized overreactions
    to, 130, 131, 132; 9/11 attacks, 6, 7,
    10, 34; police tactics as, 134–35;
    responses of authorities and,
    130–31, 132; suicide missions,
    47–48; terrorist attacks, 48; use for
    governance and social control, 30;
    Vaidya assassination, 90. See also
    beheadings; bombings; kidnap-
    pings

warriors: attitude of former, 3–4, 144–45; invulnerability illusion of, 12; underground Khalistan movement and, 3, 145; unrepentant jihadi, 31–39, 144
waterboarding, 39
West Bank, 128
women: Babbar Khalsa's prohibitions for, 89; ISIS treatment of, 67
worldview(s): conflict end and shifts in, 1; ISIS (Islamic State of Iraq and Sham), 11; of militants and cosmic war, 131; transitions of, 15–16, 16; war and shifts in, 9–10

Yassin, Ahmed, 125–26
Yazidis, 30, 37, 46

YouTube, 45–46, 46

Zabala, Francis, 159
Zaffarwal, Wassan Singh: about, 86–87, 159; Akali protests, 87–88; on Bhindranwale, 88; electoral politics and, 128, 137; on KCF, 91–92, 93–94; Khalistan Liberation Army and, 89; on Khalistan movement, 88, 94, 115, 116, 120, 123, 130, 133; on killing, 104; in Pakistan, 92–93; Panthic Committee and, 89–90; return to India, 93, 113, 137; in Switzerland, 93; on Vaidya assassination, 91
al-Zarqawi, Abu Musab, 27–28, 35, 42, 44
al-Zawahiri, Ayman, 29

Founded in 1893,
UNIVERSITY OF CALIFORNIA PRESS
publishes bold, progressive books and journals
on topics in the arts, humanities, social sciences,
and natural sciences—with a focus on social
justice issues—that inspire thought and action
among readers worldwide.

The UC PRESS FOUNDATION
raises funds to uphold the press's vital role
as an independent, nonprofit publisher, and
receives philanthropic support from a wide
range of individuals and institutions—and from
committed readers like you. To learn more, visit
ucpress.edu/supportus.